Donald Campbell

A Brighter Sunshine

A Hundred Years of the Edinburgh Royal Lyceum Theatre

D1542895

Polygon Books

First published in 1983 by Polygon Books
1 Buccleuch Place, Edinburgh EH8 9LW

The publisher acknowledges subsidy from the
Scottish Arts Council towards the publication
of this volume

ISBN 0904 919 70 6
Typeset by Edinburgh University Student
Publications Board, Edinburgh.
Reproduced from film supplied, printed and
bound by Spectrum Printing Company,
Edinburgh.

British Library Cataloguing in Publication Data
    Campbell, Donald
    A Brighter Sunshine:
    One Hundred Years of the Royal Lyceum
    1. Royal Lyceum (Edinburgh)—History
    I. Title
    792'.09413'4   PN2605.E/
    ISBN 0 904919 70 6

D2662

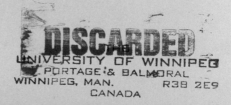

A Brighter Sunshine

I am delighted as Lord Provost to have been invited to contribute a short foreword to Donald Campbell's excellent history of the Royal Lyceum Theatre which this year celebrates its Centenary.

City Chambers,
Edinburgh, EH1 1PL.

Prior to 1883 the land upon which the Royal Lyceum stands was, in fact, occupied by another theatre. Authentic records are unfortunately very difficult to trace but it has been established that the 'old theatre' was built on the site of the original Cook's Circus.

By the Right Honourable
Tom Morgan, CBE,
The Lord Provost.

The Royal Lyceum Theatre was opened on 10th September 1883 by a notable company from the London Lyceum Theatre in a performance of William Shakespeare's "Much Ado About Nothing". The Cast that evening was headed by the distinguished Mr Henry Irving (as he then was) and Miss Ellen Terry, who were about to embark on a tour of America.

Since its opening, most of the 'greats' in the world of theatre have trod the boards at the Royal Lyceum Theatre, which is, I think, accepted by a great many actors and actresses as the finest example of Victorian theatre in the country.

Until the early 1960's the theatre was owned and managed by the firm of Howard and Wyndham Limited with the celebrated and much loved Wilson Barrett Company. Now the theatre is occupied by the resident Royal Lyceum Theatre Company which continues in the best traditions of offering throughout the year a high standard of drama and comedy to theatre lovers not only in the City of Edinburgh, but from much further afield. For a few weeks each year the theatre is taken over by our renowned Edinburgh International Festival.

I feel quite sure that the Lyceum Theatre will continue to be one of the great attractions and invaluable assets of the City of Edinburgh.

Tom Morgan
Lord Provost

Acknowledgements

Without the help, guidance and encouragement of numerous individuals and institutions, this book could never have been written. The author wishes to express his grateful thanks and appreciation to the following: Winifred Bannister, George Bruce, Bill Bryden, Jean Campbell, Dame Daphne du Maurier, the City Librarian, the staff of the Edinburgh Room at Edinburgh Central Public Library, the Edinburgh Festival Society, Messrs Faber & Faber, Tom Fleming, Tom Fidelo, Michael Grieve, Messrs Howard & Wyndham, David Hutchison, Robert James, Ludovic Kennedy, Leslie Lawton, Jimmy Leadbetter, Calum Mill, Helen Murdoch, Ruari McNeill, Donald Mackenzie, Linda Mackenney, the National Library of Scotland, Roger Savage, the Scottish Theatre Archive, Scotsman Publications, Charles Tripp and Clara Young.

Contents

Respectfully dedicated to the playgoers of Edinburgh

". . . the aim is true—
To flood with rosier colours all the past,
To picture out fresh glories and to cast
A brighter sunshine o'er our Scottish stage."

J. Lee Campbell
Prologue to First Performance
10th September, 1883

Introduction

One hundred years is a very long time. Any attempt at a comprehensive coverage of the history of the Royal Lyceum Theatre would inevitably involve the consideration of something in excess of four thousand separate productions — a task that is clearly beyond the scope of a single volume — and so, on practical grounds alone, it has been necessary to employ a degree of selectivity in the writing of this book. Selectivity, however, has not only been necessary but desirable for quite another reason.

A theatre is so much more than just a building, a collection of bricks and mortar. It is a living institution, a public forum in which the tastes, concerns, dreams and aspirations of the entire community are reflected and exposed. It follows, therefore, that the history of any theatre is capable of yielding unique insights into the life and times of the society which that theatre has served. The aim of this book — the basis upon which the selection of the material has been made — is to tell the story of the Royal Lyceum in terms of the social and cultural context of which it has formed a part.

Within this context, many influences have been at work, some transitory and no longer relevant, others permanent and enduring. The approach taken here has been to concentrate on the latter, in the hope that this will provide readers with an understanding of the reasons why the Royal Lyceum has been able to play such a vital role in the life of the community for so long.

Perhaps the most obvious influence of all has been what might be described, quite reasonably, as the 'English dimension'. When the Lyceum first opened its doors in 1883, it did so in the conscious belief that it was making a contribution to the new movement that was taking place in the English theatre at that time. All the most important developments which have taken place since — from the trail-blazing days of the great actor-managers, through the colourful period of commercial expansion and the hey-day of repertory, to the arrival of today's subsidised theatre — have been reflected in the Lyceum to such an extent that the history of this one theatre could be described, with some justice, as the history of the English Theatre in microcosm.

At the same time, of course, it is important to recognise that the Lyceum has never been an English theatre as such. Although the movement towards the creation of a distinctively Scottish Theatre is of fairly recent origin — and the Lyceum's part in this movement, until even more recently, has been minimal — there has never been a time when anyone at the Lyceum has been allowed to forget that the theatre is in Scotland. Scottish sentiments and aspirations have always had to be taken into account in the formulation of the theatre's policy and, indeed, they have on occasion been rigorously exploited. The Scottish dimension of the Lyceum's history, to say the very least, is just as important as the English one.

Geographically, of course, the Lyceum is not only situated in Scotland, but lies in the heart of Scotland's capital city. Particularly since 1947, when the Edinburgh Festival was established, this has created an additional, international dimension, with the Lyceum assuming the status and role of a major European venue for three weeks in every year. Although it is true to say that the Lyceum exhibited a European consciousness long before the Festival began — a fact which, in itself, helped to establish the Festival in Edinburgh — there is no denying that the success of the Edinburgh Festival has played a crucial part in the Lyceum's survival. The international dimension is, therefore, an extremely important one.

Most important of all, however, is the fact that the Lyceum is an Edinburgh theatre. The rich and varied history of the Edinburgh Stage, going back many centuries, has had the effect of creating an audience which has a quite definite personality of its own. The two most prominent features of this personality are a discerning

10

common sense and an absolute refusal to tolerate the merest suggestion of the second-rate. Since it is not an audience which is normally given to expressing its feelings in an extravagant manner, these qualities can too easily be mistaken for conservatism and a predictable lack of adventure. Conservative or not, however, there has never been anything predictable about the Lyceum audience. On the contrary, beneath the surface, it has often proved to be highly volatile, capable of warm appreciation on the one hand, and heart-breaking indifference on the other.

These, then, are the main components of the general context in which the Royal Lyceum Theatre has had its being for the past century. In telling the Lyceum's story in terms of this context, many interesting productions have, of necessity, escaped mention. No matter how much this is to be regretted, the fact remains that, given the length and diversity of the Lyceum's history, some kind of omission was clearly unavoidable, even though the author has made every attempt to include as much material as possible. To this end, critical discussion of individual plays has been kept to the minimum and any analysis of the complicated considerations of artistic policy has, in the main, been scrupulously avoided.

Prologue

The scene is the Royal Lyceum Theatre, Edinburgh, on the evening of the 10th September, 1883. The atmosphere is one of excited anticipation. As the handsome new safety curtain rises, there is huge and prolonged applause from a packed house of some two thousand, five hundred Edinburgh playgoers. A drop scene, designed by Fred Dangerfield, is revealed. This consists of a monochrome reproduction of a group from the Alma Tadema painting of Sappho with Alcaeus, enclosed within a drapery of dazzling blue, tinted with yellow.

Enter J. B. Howard, in full evening dress.

> *Howard:* The Spell is wrought — my chafing
> is all spent —
> "Now is the winter of my discontent"
> Made glorious summer by the sunshine here
> Of faces well-remembered, now more dear.
> Welcome, kind friends!
> *Cheers*
>   My heart is brimming o'er.
> For in your smiles and laughter, as of yore,
> I read the words that grace the good old song—
> "True, true is the liking that likes for long"
> There's something good in everything that's
> old,
> And old acquaintance never can grow cold.
> *Cheers*
> 'Twas Shakespeare in his keen and witty way,
> Who asked 'What's in a name?' — To say him
> nay
> Were rude, but in a loved and honoured name
> Is sorcery — a hostage 'tis to fame —
> And in its own deep melody is charm
> To keep traditions in our heart more warm.
> It was a wise philosophy that knew
> The groves of *Lyceum* old; but in the new
> From out whose shrine we steal Promethean
> fire,
> The ancient Thespis with new life t'inspire,
> A wizard hand has writ in letters golden —

13

Mankind to our loved art is more beholden
Than to philosophy! Irving, 'tis thine
To shed new magic over Shakespeare's line,
And with the wit that genius can devise
Conjure up worlds before a world's proud eyes.
Cheers
"What's in a name?" The *Lyceum* lives for aye,
For 'neath its shade art grew to deathless day
Tended, when fading from the ungrateful light,
By these bright souls we gladly greet tonight.
Cheers
This is the prologue to the chapter new
Of our own fortunes; and the aim is true —
To flood with rosier colours all the past,
To picture out fresh glories, and to cast
A brighter sunshine o'er our Scottish stage
That boasts its thousand heroes; every age
Is thronged with memories, braver grown with years
While rivalry with generous fire appears
To feed the sacred flame.
Cheers
   Proud of our prize,
Won in the fight before your very eyes,
A brighter garland still we'd fain disclose:-
Our own endeavours are the green, the rose
Is Wyndham —
Cheers
   While forget-me-nots entwine
For old acquaintance sake; with trophies fine
As these, I see a vista spreading bright
Down through the future's forest, and the light
Is ever in your smiles. Irving, we've here —
Cheers
Loved, of two worlds, with Ellen Terry, dear
To every pulsing heart —
Cheers
   Toole soon will wield
His mirthful wand, to which all sorrows yield;
While Clarke, as *Wellington de Boots* will come,
To prove himself the Toole of Yankeedom,
And merrier than of old; Ristori, too,
Will on these boards make us forever rue
Macbeth's foul deed; anon Miss Wallis sweet
And gracious in her presence we shall greet;
While Wilson Barrett bears a New Year's gift,
A new-born play, that will his name uplift
To honours fresh; again in Protean guise
Old Pantomime will dance before your eyes,
Taking his cue amid his merry fits
From woman's lips and woman's happier wits —
At Mrs Howard's nod, chanting with glee
Red Riding Hood's immortal history
Cheers

Enter F. W. Wyndham, similarly attired. He addresses Howard.

> *Wyndham:* As Falstaff says — "Fine words,
> brave words", my friend!
> And to their fairness can I nothing lend —
> *Cheers. Wyndham turns to audience*
> *Wyndham:* Saving in this — I am my father's
> son —
> *Loud Cheers*
> If rugged Time from out your hearts has won
> The treasures of the past, for me 'tis full
> Of dreams and mem'ries sweet —
> *Cheers*
>   your's was the school
> Where first I strutted on the mimic scene —
> Alas, poor boards, we say that they have *been*
> And are not! — 'Auld Lang Syne' is here
> tonight
> *Cheers*
> The sunshine of the olden days is bright
> Upon our hearts as when my father played;
> I'sooth, these happy times can never fade —
> They'll prove to use a neverfailing guide
> Unto your affections!
> *Howard:* Our hearts are wide
> And, like our pockets, gaping for your love —
> *Laughter*
> Which, to entice, this merry plan we've wove.
> Mercy is yours, ye critics, when your wrath
> Flashes its lightning o'er our smiling path;
> Be to us tutors kind, e'en when severe,
> And may your lightnings quicken, never sear!
> Thus with your cheers ringing a happy clime,
> In loving answer to our limping rhyme,
> We crave the boon that friends must ever
> crave,
> Forbear when we have trespassed — we'll
> enslave
> Our very will that all our thoughts may sing
> In perfect music with your own; everything
> Smiles on us now, and of your own sweet grace
> Smooth all the furrows in Dame Fortune's
> face,
> That *Lyceum* still may prove another name
> For what is best — of wit, success and fame.
> *Loud cheers and applause*

Mr Howard and Mr Wyndham take their bows and leave the stage. Curtain.

1   'Another Name for What is Best'

On the evening of the 10th September 1883, a young boy was taken into custody at Tollcross Police Station, Edinburgh. He had been in the queue in the gallery stair of the new Royal Lyceum Theatre and, apparently fearing that the house would fill up before he could gain admission, had shouted 'Fire!' in an attempt to clear a path for himself. He was charged with committing a breach of the peace, kept in the cells overnight, fined and released the next day. This little incident, obscure and unremarkable though it may seem, indicates something of the excitement that swept through the Edinburgh population on the occasion of the Lyceum's opening a hundred years ago.

This excitement originated from a number of causes, not the least of which was the fact that Henry Irving and the London Lyceum Company were to appear in the theatre for the first two weeks of its existence. Irving was the superstar of the Victorian age, his partnership with Ellen Terry being the most popular theatrical attraction of the time. For the next two weeks, they packed the theatre with performances of *Much Ado About Nothing, The Bells, The Belle's Stratagem, Hamlet, Louis XI* and *The Merchant of Venice*. They were treated to all sorts of receptions and supper parties and Irving was presented with a portrait by the Edinburgh Pen and Pencil Club, a prestigious body which included in its membership most of the leading figures in Edinburgh society. The critics raved about them. 'Never before,' wrote the drama critic of *The Scotsman* about *Much Ado About Nothing*, 'did Shakespeare's comedy receive an interpretation so adequate in essentials and in every detail so artistically complete.' All in all, the Irving/Terry combination gave the Royal Lyceum the best possible start.

It needed a good start. Theatre in

Sir Henry Irving: The greatest of all Victorian actors. He never forgot the debt he owed to the Edinburgh Stage and, in time, repaid it handsomely.

Edinburgh, then as now, was an extremely risky business. Eight years earlier, in 1875, another theatrical venture had been launched on a site immediately adjacent to that of the Lyceum — only to fail disastrously. This enterprise was the short-lived Edinburgh Theatre, a splendidly equipped and well-appointed playhouse, built for what was then an astronomical figure of £65,000. After no more than two years of operation, the Edinburgh Theatre closed and the property was sold, for less than half of its original cost, to the United Presbyterian Church. In the best traditions of the Victorian Presbyterian view of the public drama, the U.Ps. sold the furniture and fittings by public roup, pulled the theatre down and built their own Synod Hall in its place. Many years later, it became a cinema and at the time of writing it is a hole in the ground. What reasons were there to suppose, in 1883, that the Lyceum would not, before too long, share a similar fate.

The big difference between the two theatres lay in the approach of the management. To begin with, the Lyceum was built for almost a quarter of the cost of the Edinburgh Theatre, £17,000. This economy was not gained by shoddy workmanship, but by the skill of the architect, C. J. Phipps. Apart from two major alterations — one in the nineteen-thirties and another in the nineteen-seventies — the building has lasted for a hundred years. When one considers this, it is not difficult to suspect that altogether *too* much money was spent on the Edinburgh Theatre, that the management was over-extended financially and unable to cope with the competition afforded by other forms of public amusement. With the demise of the Edinburgh Theatre added to the fact that the Lyceum itself was built on a site that had previously been occupied by the popular Cooke Bros. Circus, two of the most potent sources of competition were eliminated at a stroke. More importantly, however, the new proprietors were men whose names were synonymous with theatrical success in Edinburgh at that time. Whatever had been the cause of the demise of the Edinburgh Theatre, it is quite certain that it had had nothing to do with any absence of

J. B. Howard: The senior founder of the Royal Lyceum, seen here in his most famous role, 'Rob Roy'. Although an Irishman, Howard became a specialist in playing Scott heroes.

demand on the part of the general public. What was needed was an experienced and energetic management that was capable of serving that demand. The partnership of J. B. Howard and F. W. P. Wyndham could not have been better suited to do just that.

The link between those two men had been provided by Wyndham's father, R. H. Wyndham, one of the most popular and successful actor-managers of Victorian Scotland. Wyndham Senior had first come to Edinburgh to perform under the management of William Murray at the old Theatre Royal in Shakespeare Square (the site of the present General Post Office) and had stayed on to found his own theatre, the Adelphi, in Elder Street. Initially, the Adelphi housed a stock company, a long-extinct form of theatre which served, in the absence of drama schools, as the main method by which professional actors were trained at the time. Although the company included a number of experienced professionals, most of the actors were students who were allowed to play parts in exchange for a fee to the management. The Adelphi company appears to have been a particularly efficient one, since two of the most distinguished actors of the Victorian stage, Henry Irving and John Laurence Toole, gained early experience there. In 1853, the Adelphi was destroyed by fire, was rebuilt and renamed the Queen's (in honour of Queen Victoria) and continued under that name until 1859. Murray's Theatre Royal closed in that year and the Queen's assumed the name. The Theatre Royal, Wyndham Senior's theatre, lasted for almost a century, although it seems to have been singularly cursed by the fire hazard. Within the space of twenty years, it was destroyed and rebuilt no fewer than three times — in 1863, 1875 and 1884 — and it was as a result of a fire that it finally closed in 1946. For many years, it was the leading professional theatre in Edinburgh, but after the fire of 1875, R. H. Wyndham decided that he had had enough, retired from the stage and handed the management over to his younger colleague, J. B. Howard.

At this time, Howard was thirty-three

F. W. P. Wyndham: Originally Howard's junior partner, Wyndham transformed the company into a theatrical empire. Never more than a competent actor, he always preferred production to performance.

years of age and already had a successful stage career behind him, both in Edinburgh and London. Born in the West of Ireland, he had started his working life as a clerk in a stockbroker's office in Liverpool. Having caught the acting bug, he joined the local stock company and eventually made the grade as a professional actor. After a short period in Glasgow, he came to Edinburgh for the first time in 1866, to appear at the Theatre Royal in an Irish play. The following year, he played for the first time what was to be his most popular part — the title role of *Rob Roy*. His portrayal of Scott's hero made an immediate impact, even though contemporary critics took exception to his size (he was not considered big enough to play Rob) and to the lack of authenticity in his attempts to speak Scots. Over the years, his grasp of Scots gradually improved and it must be assumed that audiences did not greatly object to his physical shortcomings, because he was to play the part many times in the years to come. Indeed, he became quite a specialist in Scottish roles: besides *Rob Roy*, he acted in (and directed productions of) *Kenilworth, The Lady of the Lake, Guy Mannering, The Heart of Midlothian* and *Old Mortality*. Apart from a three-year period between 1869 and 1872 with the Drury Lane Company in London (during which time he played Tom Burrowes in Dion Boucicault's *Formosa* and the title role in *Ivanhoe*) he spent the rest of his career in Edinburgh. His management at the Theatre Royal had been just as popular and successful as that of his predecessor's, being particularly noted for its spectacular and entertaining pantomimes. By the time the Lyceum opened, Howard was probably the best-known figure in Edinburgh theatrical life.

At twenty-nine years of age, F. W. P. Wyndham was very much the junior partner. Edinburgh born and bred, he was, like Howard and the elder Wyndham, an actor who had played all over the United Kingdom, including London. Acting, however, was not his true forte. Whereas Howard was an actor who knew how to manage, Wyndham was a manager who could be relied upon to give a competent performance when required. In the years that lay ahead, he was to lay the foundations of the Howard & Wyndham empire, a many-sided theatrical business which controlled a large number of theatres throughout the length and breadth of the British Isles. He was never *simply* a businessman, however, but rather an artist whose art happened to be theatre management. He was born in 1853, in a house above the old Adelphi theatre, one week before that first fire. For the rest of his life, he quite literally lived for the theatre, devoting all his energies to its welfare and never being completely happy unless he was involved in its activities.

These, then, were the men who founded the Royal Lyceum Theatre; practical, experienced artists and entrepreneurs, committed completely to the theatre's artistic and commercial success. Bearing this in mind, there can be no doubt that the launching of the Lyceum was planned to the last meticulous detail. Securing the services of Henry Irving to open the theatre was only the first part of a master plan to put the Lyceum well and truly on the theatrical map, to make Edinburgh, as one journalist put it at the time, 'part of the West End'.

The booking of Irving's company may seem to have been something of a coup, but the probability is that it was arranged without too much difficulty. Quite apart from any other consideration, Henry Irving loved the city of Edinburgh. 'It is indeed a city of poetry,' he once wrote enthusiastically to a friend. 'I can hardly conceive a more beautiful unity of art and nature, town and country.'

Considering the facts of Irving's early career, his affection for Edinburgh is understandable. Born John Henry Brodribb in the Somerset village of Keinton Mandeville in 1838, he had embarked upon a stage career only after the greatest of difficulties. As a child he had had a passion for mimicry and recitation, but suffered badly from a stammer which might very easily have prevented him from indulging it. Luckily, however, he attended the City Commercial School in London, where the headmaster, Dr Pinches, was enlightened enough to encourage him to use

23

elocution to conquer his impediment. On leaving school, he continued his interest by taking part in amateur theatricals while working as a clerk during the day. At the same time, he made the acquaintance of an actor called William Hoskins who, besides giving him daily acting lessons, introduced him to Samuel Phelps of Saddlers Wells, the leading actor of his day. The advice that Phelps gave to Irving has become quite famous. 'Sir,' said Phelps, 'do not go on the stage; it is an ill-requited profession.'

The young Irving, however, was not to be put off either by this or by the hostility of his family. As a stern Methodist, his mother held the firm belief that the profession of play-actor was as good as a ticket to hell, and she did everything in her power to dissuade her son from an acting career. Armed with a letter of introduction from Hoskins and the unexpected windfall of £100 (a gift from a sympathetic uncle) with which to buy his properties, Irving turned his back on his family, leaving home permanently for a life on the stage. This was the first example of the ruthless determination that was to characterise his career.

His first engagement was (coincidentally enough) at the Royal Lyceum Theatre in Sunderland. This very nearly ended in disaster. In his first featured role, that of Cleomenes in *The Winter's Tale*, he dried up completely and was hissed off the stage. Although the manager of the theatre and some of the older actors helped him to rebuild his confidence, it was with some relief that he left Sunderland for Edinburgh, where R. H. Wyndham had offered him an engagement at the old Theatre Royal in Shakespeare Square.

At this time, Wyndham was in the course of rebuilding his own theatre after the fire of 1853 and had taken over the management of Murray's theatre for the last two years of its existence. When Irving arrived in Edinburgh, he was nineteen years old, raw, inexperienced, and still suffering from the effects of his traumatic humiliation at Sunderland. When he left, two and a half years later, he had played over four hundred parts of all descriptions and had made a name for himself with Edinburgh audiences. It must have been the happiest time in Irving's youth and he never forgot the debt he owed to the Edinburgh stage. In time, he was to repay it handsomely.

After ten years of playing with stock companies all over the British Isles, Irving finally made his breakthrough in London, playing the part of Rawdon Scudamore in Dion Boucicault's *The Two Lives of Mary Leigh*. His greatest success, however, was to come some four years later, when Hezekiah Bateman, an American theatre manager, engaged him at the Royal Lyceum Theatre in London. He played here, for the first time, the part of Matthias in a play called *The Bells*.

The Bells is not a great play. In fact, it is not even a good play. It is never performed now and, indeed, owes its fame solely to the fact that it was the perfect vehicle for Irving's art. Based on a French play, *Le Juif Polonais*, it tells the story of a wealthy man who had, fifteen years earlier when poor, robbed and murdered a Polish Jew during a snowstorm. The man, Matthias, is haunted by his crime and in the last act, which is virtually a monologue, he dies of self-induced terror. Irving's performance in this role became so famous that audiences would applaud instantaneously when he walked on the stage, not just politely (as was then the custom) but in what Ellen Terry's son, Gordon Craig, has described as a 'hurricane'.

We are indebted to Gordon Craig for a detailed description of Irving's acting in *The Bells*. In his biography of the great actor, published in 1930, Craig describes a scene in the play in which the night of the murder has just been mentioned.

> Irving was buckling his second shoe, seated, and leaning over it with his two long hands stretched down over the buckles. We suddenly saw these fingers stop their work; the crown of the head suddenly seemed to glitter and become frozen — and then, at the pace of the slowest and most terrified snail, the two hands, still motionless and dead, were seen to be coming up the side of the leg . . . the whole torso of the man, also seeming frozen, was drawing up and back, as it would straighten a little and to lean a

little against the back of the chair in which he was seated.

Once in that position — motionless — eyes fixed ahead of him and fixed on us all — there he sat for the space of ten or twelve seconds, which I can assure you seemed to us like a lifetime, and then said — and said in a voice deep and overwhelmingly beautiful, 'Oh, you were talking of that — were you?'.

The applause with which Irving's performance was inevitably received became almost part of the play — in another invaluable phrase of Craig's 'power responded to power'.

It was this power that the audiences at Royal Lyceum in Edinburgh experienced during that first week of the theatre's existence in September 1883. Added to this power was the charm and beauty and sheer personality of Ellen Terry. Although these two weeks constituted her first appearance in Edinburgh, there can be no doubt that she won the hearts of Edinburgh audiences just as completely as she did elsewhere. Of all Victorian actors and actresses, she must be accounted the most charismatic. Although many contemporary commentators have written of Irving's almost hypnotic hold over his audiences, there is no way that anyone presently living can experience his personality. Fascinating though he is, Irving exists in the modern consciousness as a character in a history book: we know as much and as little about him as we do of Gladstone. In a curious way, however, Ellen Terry's personality lives on, more than a century after her death. There is a hint of it in Charles Reade's famous description of her.

Ellen Terry is an enigma. Her eyes are pale, her nose rather long, her mouth nothing in particular. Complexion a delicate brick-dust, her hair rather like tow. Yet somehow she is *beautiful*. Her expression *kills* any pretty face you see beside her. Her figure is lean and bony; her hand masculine in size and form. Yet she is a pattern of fawn-like grace. Whether in movement or repose, grace pervades the hussy.

There are, of course, many photographs, paintings and drawings (particularly those done by her first husband, G. F. Watts) of Ellen

Terry which tell us a great deal more of her beauty. The warmth of her personality, however, shines through at its most radiant in her correspondence and her diaries. Her partnership with Irving was the most famous that the theatre has ever known and, although this is not the place to discuss their personal relationship, it is quite obvious that she loved him very much. The following is a description of Irving, taken from a diary that Ellen Terry kept in 1895, which tells us a great deal more about her than it does about him.

> A splendid figure and his face very noble. A superb brow: rather small dark eyes which can at moments become immense, and hang like a bowl of dark liquid, with light shining through; a most refined curving Roman nose, strong and delicate in line; and *cut clean* (as all his features); a smallish mouth, and full of the most wonderful teeth, even at 55; lips most delicate and refined — firm, firm, firm — and with a rare smile of the most exquisite beauty, and quite-not-to-be described kind. (He seems almost ashamed of his smile, even in very private life, and will withdraw it at once in public.) His chin, and the line from ear to chin is firm, extremely delicate, and very strong and clean defined. He has an ugly ear! Large, flabby, ill-cut, and pasty-looking, pale and lumpy. His hair is superb: beautiful in 1867, when I first met him, when it was blue-black like a raven's wing, it is even more splendid now when it is liberally streaked with white. . . .

When Ellen Terry wrote these words, she was forty-eight years of age and had known Irving for twenty-seven years. Their partnership, which had begun seventeen years earlier, had long passed the peak of its achievement and would end, four years later, in 1899. That she could still write of him with all the enthusiasm and impish delight of a young girl tells us, not just of the devotion she felt for Irving, but of the way in which *she* felt devotion. Eighty-eight years later, one can still sense her warmth and charm.

In September 1883, the Irving/Terry partnership was at the height of its popularity. On the Monday morning of the second week of their

engagement at the Lyceum, the Edinburgh press proudly announced that the theatre's takings for the previous Saturday night (when Irving was playing in *The Bells*) had exceeded the largest amount ever taken at any theatre in Britain, 'in or out of London', with the single exception of Old Drury Lane. Partly, no doubt, this was due to the fact that the management had taken advantage of Irving's engagement to raise seat prices to double their usual rate. (A seat in the dress circle, for instance, would normally cost five shillings in those days, being the most expensive seat in the house. While Irving was in the theatre, this was raised to ten shillings and sixpence.) Even so, it was a great achievement for a new Edinburgh theatre. Irving, who had already donated £1,000 out of his own pocket to the cost of building the theatre, must surely have felt that, in financial terms at least, he had come close to repaying the debt he owed the Wyndhams for his early experience.

Overleaf

CARL ROSA OPERA COMPANY.

NADESHDA & MANON

LYCEUM THEATRE, EDINBURGH,

F — — Nights, Commencing November 9th.

TOOLE

TOOLE AS THE GREAT

TAY KIN

Tom Merry Lith
WEST SQUARE
LONDON S.E.

The debt, however, was repaid in terms which were of much greater significance. For many years afterwards, the Edinburgh public looked upon Henry Irving and his Lyceum Company as being uniquely their own. In the press reports of his first American tour — which followed immediately after the Edinburgh engagement — no attempt was made to inform readers that the 'Lyceum Company' referred to the Royal Lyceum, London, and not the Royal Lyceum, Edinburgh. Twelve years later, this disguise was still in evidence in the 'local boy makes good' tone of the reports that Henry Irving had been knighted. Irving, no doubt, did not greatly mind about any of this — there can have been few places that stood higher in his affections than Edinburgh — but it is difficult not to suspect that this was all part of Howard and Wyndham's strategy for the Lyceum. Irving himself, indeed, might have been in league with them in this respect. Both men were his friends — apart from his obvious connection with Wyndham, he had become friendly with Howard during the latter's time at Drury Lane — and he was anxious to do everything in his power to help them make the Edinburgh Lyceum 'another name for what is best'.

Be that as it may, the fact remains that Irving, whether he intended to do so or not, had placed an imprimatur of lasting quality on the new venture. As recently as 1965, Charles Graves, writing of the theatre's beginnings in *The Third Statistical Account of Scotland*, described the Lyceum as having been 'opened in 1883 by Sir Henry Irving' as if the great Victorian actor had been the original proprietor! There is no doubt that this association with Irving proved of great assistance to the management in the early days of the Lyceum's life.

In one respect, however, Irving's appearance at the theatre created something of a problem in the short term. The immediate result of that first season had been a sensation of such proportions that it was clear that any following season ran the risk of being an anti-climax.

Mr Howard and Mr Wyndham, however, had thought of this.

J. L. Toole: 'Dull must be the person who can fail to enjoy Mr Toole'. Toole was to comedy what Irving was to serious drama.

33

ROYAL LYCEUM THEATRE,
MONDAY, DECEMBER 26,
AND EVERY EVENING.

"and Saxon,
I am Roderick Dhu"

LADY OF THE LAKE

2 The New Theatre

The theatre of the early eighteen-eighties was a very different place from the theatre that we know today. With no competition from broadcasting and the cinema, audiences were much larger and, on the whole, much more knowledgeable. Performances were much longer. It was not unusual for as many as three separate plays to be performed in a single evening. People often came to the theatre straight from work, bringing their own refreshments, to sit on the hard wooden benches of the pit or the gallery. In the stalls and the dress circle, where evening dress was obligatory, there was a quite separate audience whose reactions to the play would often be quite different from that of the cheaper seats. Both audiences, however, were extremely vociferous in either appreciation or censure. Since curtain calls were taken at the end of every act of a play, they had ample opportunity to let the performers know their feelings. Most of the theatres were lit by gas (electric light was the Lyceum's most modern feature) and there were no artificial aids of any kind. An actor had to be heard clearly at the very back of the house and, if he could not be, he very quickly found out about it.

We would be quite mistaken, however, if we were to believe that this noisy, knowledgeable, thriving theatre was an old-established institution. In many important respects, it was quite a new phenomenon. Before discussing the production strategy that was to guide the management of the Lyceum for the next thirty years, this new phenomenon has to be examined more closely, in order that the context of that strategy can be properly understood.

Up until the middle of the nineteenth century, most theatres in the British Isles conformed to a very strict pattern which had its basis in the stock company. As has been already

The Lady of the Lake: One of the many successful adaptations of Scott classics to be seen at the Lyceum during Howard's time.

mentioned, these stock companies provided a training ground for young actors, but that was not their prime purpose. Collectively, they formed a circuit for leading actors who would tour the country from end to end, playing the same parts in different places, supported by the local actors of the stock company. Inevitably, the repertoire was dominated by 'stock' plays, in which the local actors specialised in 'stock' characters. The names of these characters will be instantly familiar, since they have become part of the English language. Each stock play had a leading man and a leading lady (played by the visitor usually), a juvenile lead in both sexes, a low comedian and a chambermaid. In addition to these, there were a number of Walking Ladies and Gentlemen, later to be known as Supernumeraries or simply Supers. Quite obviously, this system — in which, incidentally, actors were extremely poorly paid — was not conducive to work of any kind of artistic quality. Although the theatre could survive under such conditions, its standing as an art form was very, very low. Socially, too, the theatre was despised, being considered, even in England, as little better than an ale-house or a brothel. In Scotland, of course, the distinction was, in those days, even more difficult to make.

Most theatre historians agree that the change in the theatre's fortunes began in the eighteen-sixties and can be pinned down to one particular event. A young actress called Marie Wilton, described by Charles Dickens as 'the cleverest girl I have ever seen on the stage', had become dissatisfied with the parts she was being offered and determined to do something about it. With £1,000 she had borrowed from her brother-in-law, she took over a theatre off the Tottenham Court Road in London. This theatre, officially known as the Queen's, had become so run-down that it had earned the local nickname of 'the Dusthole'. Marie Wilton transformed it completely. She had the theatre cleaned and redecorated, installed new seats and new furniture, created an entirely new *style* of theatre. In time, Marie Wilton was joined by a young actor called Sydney 'Squire'

Bancroft (whom she later married) and a playwright called T. W. Robertson. On the 11th November 1865, a new comedy by Robertson called *Society* opened at Marie Wilton's theatre, now renamed the Prince of Wales, and the new era in the English-speaking theatre began.

The importance of the Bancrofts and Tom Robertson cannot be overstated. As Frances Donaldson says in her book *The Actor Managers*, they created not only 'a revolution in theatrical productions, but also a revolution in theatrical customs'. In terms of style, they were the first to introduce modern scenic effects. Although they were not the first to use real furniture, ceilings and doors on their sets, they were the first to make this standard practice in their productions.

At the same time, a very important technological development created a new situation which was to lead, in time, to the death of the stock circuit. The coming of the railways made it possible for entire companies to go on tour. Instead of simply seeing a famous actor in a performance of a famous role, audiences throughout Britain were given the opportunity, for the first time, of seeing the entire London production. The age of the great actor-managers, which was to dominate the theatre for the next three decades, had begun.

Howard and Wyndham were, of course, well aware of these new developments and were anxious to exploit them — indeed, had already begun to do so at the Theatre Royal. The new theatre, however, was to be run on a policy which would be based on the new circumstances from the very beginning. In the next thirty years, all the great actor-managers played the Lyceum, which became one of their most important dates.

The first company to arrive after Irving was led by an actress called Ada Cavendish. Unlike Irving, Cavendish did not present a programme of plays, but presented one play for an entire season. This was *The New Magdalen* by Wilkie Collins, first produced at the Olympic Theatre in London in 1873. This play, which was probably Collins' greatest commercial success in the theatre, tells the story of a 'fallen woman' and her rehabilitation through the good offices of a noble clergyman. Although it was originally a novel, it seems that this very Victorian blend of melodrama and morality was more successful on the stage. Not only was Ada Cavendish (described by Collins as having 'more of the divine fire in her than any other living English actress') to tour in it, on and off, for the next twenty years, but it was translated into German, Dutch and Russian and seen, in these languages respectively, in Berlin, The Hague and Moscow, besides touring America. The fact that Mercy Merrick, the central character of the play, is a prostitute may seem to make the play's presentation a bold and adventurous move in Victorian Edinburgh, but in fact it was very much in line with a new climate of opinion towards the theatre that was very evident in the city at the time.

An example of this new atmosphere can be seen in an event that took place a few weeks later. In those days, it was the practice to have a public holiday, in the form of a fast day, immediately prior to the three-monthly communion — presumably in order to give communicants some time to prepare for the sacrament. On the evening of this fast day, all theatres were closed, a fact that displeased their managements not a little. At the same time, the institution of this fast day — reeking, as it does, of popery — could not have found much favour in the eyes of some of the more hard-line Presbyterians. On Thursday, October 25th, 1883, a most unusual event took place in the Chaplaincy Centre of Edinburgh University.

Styled a 'sacred meeting', the event was chaired by one of the most colourful of Edinburgh academics, Professor John Stuart Blackie, who described the whole affair as a 'wonderful, even miraculous, meeting'. The Reverend Dr John Kay of Argyle Place United Presbyterian Church gave a lecture on 'The Literary Beauty of the Book of Psalms' and there was a choral contribution from his church choir. At the same time, there was a selection of instrumental pieces from a section of the Lyceum Orchestra and a visiting Bavarian band, followed by selected readings from the poetry of Shakespeare, Longfellow and Burns, given by J. B. Howard, actor and manager of the Lyceum Theatre. Admission was sixpence a head, with an additional sixpence being charged if the customer required a cushion. By any standards, it must have been a most amazing affair.

After the initial musical items and readings, Professor Blackie gave an address from the chair. Poet, classicist and Scottish patriot, Blackie was an accomplished public performer and a devotee of the theatre. He was obviously overjoyed at the nature of the meeting and made an impassioned speech on the relationship between Church and the Drama, the greater part of which was published, in a more substantial form, in his *Notes of a Life* (edited by A. Stodart Walker, 1910). The following is a short extract.

> I say now, in all seriousness, let the clergy as individuals and collectively as a Church come forward and publicly patronise all innocent amusements, especially theatres. Unless the God of Nature and the God of the Bible be two different Dieties — which, I think, Bishop Butler proved triumphantly they are not — then the drama is fundamentally from God as much as the sermon, and the stage is a divine institution no less than the pulpit. If so, the Christian churches are bound either to get up a separate sacred drama for themselves, after the manner of some well-known pieces of Metastasio, acted at Vienna during the passion week, or, what I think in every way preferable, to break down boldly the middle wall of partition that has been artificially raised in this country between the pulpit and the stage, and to enter generously into an agreement with those most respectable persons who preside over dramatic entertainments in this city, that they will give their moral and personal support to all stage representations which either provide innocent amusement or furnish a salutary moral stimulant to the people.

The true spirit of the meeting, however, is revealed by the press reports of the speaker who followed Professor Blackie. This was the Reverend John Kay of Argyle Place Church, possibly the most intriguing of the participants. Kay was a hard-line defender of Presbyterian orthodoxy, a teetotaller and a rigid moralist. This did not mean, however, that he lacked a sense of humour. As he stepped forward to speak, he noticed that Professor Blackie had left his stick on the table. Picking it up, he turned to the audience and cried, 'Lo! I have captured the club of Hercules!' Amid laughter, Blackie explained that it wasn't a club, but a kail-runt that came from the Channel Islands, where cabbages grew to enormous size, due to the fact that the Islands had Home Rule.

Kay's lecture was conducted in this spirit of levity, but retained the serious argument that the Psalms of David had more literary value than any modern poetry. During the course of the lecture, passages of illustration were read by J. B. Howard. At one point, however, Kay insisted on reading himself. This was not a psalm, but the old Scots ballad 'O, waly, waly, up the bank'. Kay asked the audience not to applaud this particular reading, because he did not want anyone outside the hall to think 'that we're having a time to ourselves in here'. It is safe to assume that this remark was made tongue-in-cheek (they were, after all, having 'a time' to themselves, and no one was doing more to encourage it than Kay) but his reason for reading the ballad is altogether more characteristic of the old Scots divine. 'Mr Howard can't read Scots,' he declared bluntly. Since the audience had, earlier on in the evening, heard Howard read *Scots Wha Hae*, this was hardly a tactful remark!

Despite hostile criticism from the press — the *Edinburgh Courant* attacked all parties, but especially the Rev. Dr Kay for commercializing the fast day — this meeting must be adjudged a great success from the point of view of the Lyceum. Apart from anything else, it showed quite clearly that the theatre had a part to play in the respectable life of the city. Were it not for this fact, it is doubtful whether the theatre would have been able to have followed such a varied and ambitious policy during the first years of its operation.

After the Cavendish company, the next most important visitor was the great Victorian comedian, J. L. Toole, appearing in a comedy called *A Fool and His Money*. Like Irving, Toole had a special affection for Edinburgh, having worked in R. H. Wyndham's stock company in his youth. He was the most popular comedian of his day, enjoying the same status in that sphere as Irving did in the field of tragedy. The affection in which he was held by his audiences can be seen in this extract from an *Edinburgh Courant* article of the time, which appeared cryptically under the signature 'A Voice from the Pit':

> Dull must be the person who can fail to enjoy Mr Toole. It is not aesthetic, but it is natural and delightful to think that Mr Toole must have given more hearty, innocent amusement to a greater number of his fellow-creatures than any man alive. There is fun in everything he does. . . . Mr Toole is a man who would make Heraclitus himself hotch with laughter.

Toole's great speciality was the satirical sending-up of contemporary drama, particularly melodrama. Many years later, when the controversy over the first English productions of Ibsen was at its height, he was encouraged by Irving to commission a young Scottish novelist to write a one-act skit on the plays of the great Norwegian dramatist. The result, *Ibsen's Ghost*, was the first play by J. M. Barrie to be given a professional production. Barrie's first full-length play, *Walker, London* (the title taken from one of Toole's cockney catchphrases), was also written for Toole and became one of the last successes of the great comedian's long career. That career had been encouraged at the outset by another great writer, Charles Dickens, who helped Toole to get his first job in the theatre, playing low comedy in Dublin. Later, Toole created the role of Bob Cratchit in the stage version of *A Christmas Carol*. Toole's visit in 1883 was the first of many he was to make to the Lyceum.

Rather less successful — although no less popular as far as Edinburgh audiences were concerned — was the company which followed Toole into the Lyceum. This was led by an actress called Miss Wallis, described at the time as 'the best

Rosalind on the British stage'. The Edinburgh press drooled over Miss Wallis, articles about her appearing daily during her visit. Like all the great actor-managers, Miss Wallis was the complete theatrical, featuring in all departments of the company's work. Her schedule for the week's performance, indeed, is quite breathtaking. On Monday, she played in *As You Like It*, on Tuesday *Measure for Measure*, on Wednesday *Cymbeline*, on Thursday it was back to *As You Like It*, on Friday *For Wife and State* (a new play that she had written and directed herself) and on Saturday *Romeo and Juliet*. Somewhat ecstatically, the drama critic of *The Scotsman* wrote of the new play that 'so far as Edinburgh can give an imprimatur of fame, its future is secure. We shall be greatly surprised indeed if *For Wife and State* does not make some noise in the dramatic world ere long.' Unfortunately, Edinburgh's 'imprimatur of fame' did not prove good enough on this occasion. As far as the author has been able to discover, *For Wife and State* was never heard of again.

The local press were rather less ecstatic about a company that came into the theatre a few weeks later. This was led by Genevieve Ward and W. H. Vernon and played for a week in *The Queen's Favourite*, an adaptation from the French of Eugene Scribe. According to *The Scotsman*, Miss Ward could 'scarcely be said to have carried the house with her. A certain monotony of intonation and a tendency to magnify the disagreeableness of a sufficiently disagreeable character marred the effect of an apparently well-studied part.' W. H. Vernon seems to have made a more favourable impression, but perhaps the most important aspect of this production was the introduction to Edinburgh audiences of a young actress called Janet Achurch. Some twenty-three years later, in 1906, Miss Achurch returned to the Lyceum in what was possibly her most famous role — that of Nora in the first English version of *A Doll's House*. Genevieve Ward is chiefly remembered today for the fact that she was the first actress to be created a Dame for her services to the stage.

It is interesting to note that of the first

half-dozen actor-managers to play the Lyceum, no fewer than four of them were women — apart from Cavendish, Wallis and Ward, Kate Vaughan's company played for a week in October in a new version of Wycherley's *The Country Wife* (renamed *The Country Girl*). The most interesting actress of all, however, arrived the following month. This was the great Italian tragedienne, Adelaide Ristori, a veteran of the old stock circuit, who was making a farewell tour of Britain, prior to her retirement from the stage. Famed for her portrayal of Lady Macbeth — her performance in the sleep-walking scene was regarded as being without equal — Madame Ristori probably acted with a local cast, since she was not one of the new breed of actor-managers. The records are unclear on this point — *The Scotsman* simply declares, somewhat enigmatically that 'of the rest of the cast, not much need be said' — and there is similar uncertainty about the language in which she played. Presumably this was English, but we cannot take that for granted. Six months later, another famous Italian actor, Tomasso Salvini, appeared at the Lyceum in a production of *Othello*, playing the role of the Moor in Italian. He was supported by a local cast which included J. B. Howard as Iago (who considered this to be the most exciting performance in his acting career), all the other actors playing in English. If this seems odd to modern ears — although, when one thinks of the play, it makes eminent sense — it should be remembered in that earlier, better-educated age, such things were possible.

Even in those days, however, it was not possible to fill the theatre all year round with serious drama. Although audiences were much larger, competition from the theatres in the East End of the city — the Theatre Royal and the Royal Princess — was much fiercer. From the beginning, the Lyceum management were at pains to create a varied and eclectic play policy. In the early years, besides the acting companies, there were visits from many burlesques and popular comics. Perhaps the most outstanding of those was the American comedian J. S. Clarke, described by Mr Howard as 'the Toole of Yankeedom'. One suspects that this description is not strictly accurate, since Clarke seems to have been a much more visual comedian than Toole, who was really a comedy actor. 'His military strut,' commented *The Scotsman*, 'is perpetually at variance with the startled look in his eyes.' Among other famous slapsticks and burlesques to visit the theatre were the Vokes Family, very popular throughout Britain and America, but in their last years at that time.

At the other end of the theatrical scale, there was opera. Among a number of companies to play regular seasons at the Lyceum, perhaps the most popular was the Carl Rosa Opera company, later the Royal Carl Rosa Opera Company. Founded some ten years before the Lyceum, the Carl Rosa was to visit the theatre more or less annually for the next forty years. When the first season was announced, the music critic of *The Scotsman* welcomed it as follows.

> The public can rely on Mr Carl Rosa's determination that his company shall be of the first quality and, whether in individual merit and excellence or in general completeness and detail, it is without doubt an admitted fact that his success is assured and public support a matter of course. He has spent great strength and means in the object of establishing as far as possible a national institution.

For once, at least, *The Scotsman* prophesy proved to be accurate. The Carl Rosa Opera Company never failed to be successful at the Lyceum.

Success in those days, of course, had to be commercial as well as critical — and the great money-spinner, then as now, was pantomime. The Howard & Wyndham pantomime tradition, which continues at the King's Theatre to the present day (at the time of writing, no fewer than eight Edinburgh pantomimes have been hired out to theatres all over the United Kingdom) began at the Lyceum in December 1883 with a production of *Little Red Riding Hood*. This lavish production which drew high praise from the *Edinburgh Courant*, *The Scotsman* and the *London Telegraph*, ran for three months, something of a record at the time, knocking out all competition completely.

When the Theatre Royal, in a desperate attempt to counter the success of the Lyceum, inserted the slogan 'The Young People's Pantomime' in the advertising for their own show, *Bluebeard*, the Lyceum struck back immediately with the following slogan.

The Young People's Pantomime!
    The Parent's Pantomime!
        The Middle-Aged Pantomime!
            The Old People's Pantomime!
                Everybody's Pantomime!

Ironically enough, the Theatre Royal was to have its revenge very shortly after *Little Red Riding Hood* had closed. To add to the irony, this revenge was exacted from a company whose name, some sixty years later, would become synonymous with the Lyceum Theatre in the minds of the Edinburgh public. On the 18th March 1884, the Wilson Barrett Company arrived with a new play called *Claudian,* by Wills and Herman.

Wilson Barrett remains one of the most fascinating of all Victorian actor-managers. Unlike Irving and Tree and so many others, he was never to gain the respectability and acceptance of a knighthood and he was never, like them, to become identified with any one theatre. Instead, he barnstormed his way across Britain and America, making and losing several fortunes as he did so. A fine actor and an astute director, he was more of a gambler than most when it came to business. Towards the end of his career, when he found himself stranded and penniless in America, he sat down and wrote a play that was to restore his fortunes entirely. This play, *The Sign of the Cross* was a spectacular religious drama, in the Wilson Barrett mould. Melodrama, especially large-scale melodrama, was his stock-in-trade.

Claudian was very much the kind of play in which the Wilson Barrett Company excelled. Co-written by W. G. Wills (dubbed by Bernard Shaw Irving's 'resident playwright', probably the first time that expression was used) and Henry 'Daddy' Herman (who had collaborated with Henry Arthur Jones in another Wilson Barrett success, *The Silver King*), the play is set in

45

the Byzantine period and tells the story of a young libertine, Claudian, who murders a priest. As a result of this crime, Claudian is visited by a two-fold curse: he will never grow any older and everyone he loves will be destroyed. In short, it was exactly the kind of play that Victorian audiences loved. Apart from the obvious appeal to Christian sentiments, the high-point of the play is an earthquake scene which, although commonplace by modern standards, sent contemporary audiences into a frenzy of excitement. In London, *Claudian* had been a huge success — John Ruskin confessed that he was so fascinated by it that he had gone to see it three times — and there was every reason to believe that it would be given a similar reception in Edinburgh. That this failed to happen had little to do with either the play or the performance — although it does seem that the earthquake scene was less effective in Edinburgh than it had been in London — but it was simply due to the fact that the production coincided with a play called *Through My Heart First* which was attracting large audiences at the Theatre Royal. Little is known about this play, except for the fact that it was a sentimental, romantic love story, written by an Edinburgh author, J. M. Campbell.

This latter fact is most important to our understanding of the theatrical atmosphere in which the early management of the Lyceum had to operate. The theatre then, of course, was not in any sense a Scottish theatre — this concept, one might even say ideal, did not begin to appear in Scotland until some thirty years later — but neither could it be said to be an English theatre either — except, of course, in terms of its language. It was a theatre, however, in which the perceptions and susceptibilities of the audience were paramount. Both Howard and Wyndham knew that, whatever enthusiasm they might have for the new theatre that was emerging from London, they would ignore Scottish sentiments at their peril — and it would never have occurred to either of them to do so. On the contrary, they exploited these sentiments whenever they could.

The recent, successful pantomime, for instance, had not only featured a 'Scotch dame' in the shape of the Scottish actor and comedian J. B. Gordon, but had included, as its most spectacular set-piece, a 'Tribute to Scotland' in the form of a transformation scene in which Robert Burns was presented with a cluster of laurel leaves by the fairies! On a more serious level, both men would have been fully acquainted, through Wyndham's father, with the work that had been done at the old Theatre Royal in Shakespeare Square by the management of William Murray. As Donald Mackenzie has shown in his fine study of this management, *Scotland's First National Theatre*, Murray made the first really substantial attempt to establish a repertoire of Scottish plays. In addition to presenting adaptations from the novels of Sir Walter Scott — for many decades afterwards, the term 'Scottish play' really meant 'Scott-ish play' — he commissioned and, indeed, wrote a number of new plays, the most successful of which was probably *Cramond Brig*.

Most celebrated of all, however, was the Scott classic, *Rob Roy*. It is significant that, when the Theatre Royal suffered yet another fire in 1884, this was the play that the Lyceum chose to present in a benefit performance to raise money for the Theatre Royal's manager, John Hislop. On this occasion, the title role was taken, not by J. B. Howard (who played Rashleigh Osbaldistone) but by A. D. McNeill, manager of the Princess Theatre. Mrs Howard played Helen MacGregor and J. B. Gordon was Baillie Nicol Jarvie, his pronunciation of the Scots (or 'Doric' as they were wont to call the language in those days) being described as 'irreproachable'. After the first night — which raised, incidentally, a sum in excess of £200 for the Theatre Royal — the play was kept in production for a two-week run, Howard resuming the role of Rob. Many years later, this play was to feature in one of the most glittering occasions that the Lyceum has ever known, during the State Visit of King Olaf of Norway in 1962.

The 1884 production of *Rob Roy* followed a season of plays by Howard and Wyndham's own resident company. Three of these — *The Shaughran*, *Formosa* and *The Colleen Bawn*

— were by Dion Boucicault, but the season had opened with a play by Tom Taylor, *The Ticket-of-Leave Man*. Since Boucicault and Taylor were the two most successful modern playwrights of their period — which was, moreover, almost over for both of them — this season could hardly be described as being in the least experimental or even speculative. It was indicative, however, of yet another strand in the policy of the Lyceum management. Resourceful managers though they were, neither Howard or Wyndham had set up in business merely to become booking agents for London companies. Apart from the fact that they realised the importance of creating a definite house style for the Lyceum, both men (but especially Howard) had a deep need to perform. For the next twenty years or so, the resident company performed a season of plays in the summer months.

The eclectic policy that the original management created — including as it did classic and contemporary drama from both the resident and visiting companies, pantomime, burlesque, opera on the one hand and low comedy on the other — was to stand the Lyceum in good stead for the best part of the next three decades. During this time, all the great names of the British theatre appeared regularly on the Lyceum stage. The following list of names, although representative, is certainly not all-inclusive. Companies led by actors included those of Sir Henry Irving, J. L. Toole, Sir George Alexander, Sir Charles Wyndham, Sir Charles Hawtrey, Sir John Hare, Edward Compton, Sir Frank Benson, Sir Herbert Beer-bohm Tree, Sir Johnston Forbes Robertson, Wilson Barrett, Osmond Tearle, Fred Terry and Sir John Martin Harvey. Actresses who either appeared with these companies or led their own included Dame Madge Robertson (Mrs Kendal), Mrs Patrick Campbell, Dame Ellen Terry, Dame Genevieve Ward, Dorothea Baird, Violet and Irene Vanburgh, Ada Cavendish, Marie Compton, Julia Neilson, Marie Lohr and Lily Langtry.

This was the time, more than any other before or since, in which the theatre came most fully into its own. It was truly a golden age,

Sir John Martin Harvey: One of the most popular of the actor-managers, Martin Harvey had a long association with the Lyceum. He was a young man in Irving's company and played the theatre for the last time in the thirties.

during which the theatre was transformed from a low and artless amusement, and returned to its rightful place as once of the very highest forms of human expression. Yet this transformation was achieved completely without any sense of elitism, snobbery or social division. On the contrary, the theatre became the art-form that united classes. W. MacQueen Pope, in his prologue of his book *The Footlights Flickered* (Herbert Jenkins, 1959), describes the experience of pre-1914 theatre-going quite brilliantly.

> A visit to a play was No 1 'Evening Out'. It was something to which the audience looked forward and for which they put on their best clothes. Playgoers not in evening dress were unwelcome in the boxes, stalls and dress circle, and in certain theatres those so improperly dressed were refused admission. Playgoing was not a matter of 'dropping in' — you did that at the pictures or the music-hall — and for those who did not want to 'dress' there were the pit and the gallery and the upper circle. The theatre catered for everybody. But mostly the theatre was looked upon as being worth a bit of trouble. One felt, when visiting an actor-manager's theatre, that one was his guest . . . the theatre was important, part of one's life, a thing of excitement and memories.

This state of affairs did not exactly come to an end in 1914, but it received a very severe knock. Changed circumstances, as we shall see, enforced a change in policy and many theatres, who either could not or would not adjust to the change, simply failed to survive. That the Lyceum was better prepared than most was due, in part, to an accident of fate which had taken place almost twenty years earlier.

In 1895, the company of Howard & Wyndham Ltd. was formed, to run the Lyceum, the recently acquired Theatre Royal in Edinburgh and a similarly named theatre in Glasgow, together with the Royalty Theatre in Glasgow which had been taken on lease. Mr Michael Simons was the chairman, but the company was to be run by the joint managing directors, J. B. Howard and F. W. P. Wyndham. A matter of weeks after the company had been formed, J. B. Howard suffered a stroke and died. He was fifty-four years of age, an active, talented, charismatic personality who had, more than anyone else, been responsible for the establishment of the Lyceum as an integral part of Edinburgh life. Appropriately enough, he died in his office at the theatre.

This versatile and dedicated actor-manager (whose real name, incidentally, was Michael Hoban) made a contribution to the Scottish stage that has never really been recognised. As a producer, the work of his resident company encouraged much local talent and allowed the Lyceum to develop its own theatrical personality. As a manager and impresario, he brought the finest companies of his time to Edinburgh and developed, in the field of pantomime, considerable skills which he unselfishly passed on — first to Wyndham, then, through him to Stewart Cruikshank — thereby establishing an Edinburgh theatrical tradition which still flourishes today. It is as an actor, however, that Howard would probably most wish to be remembered. As an example of his ability in this sphere, one need look no further than his playing of Iago in the 1884 production of *Othello* which was mentioned earlier. On that occasion, an excited playgoer, stirred by Salvini's performance as the Moor, rushed up to the stage during the curtain call and presented the great Italian actor with a laurel wreath. Without uttering a single word, Salvini walked across the stage and placed the gift on Howard's head. Howard later admitted that this had been the proudest moment of his acting career.

With Howard's death, authority passed from an actor who knew how to manage to a manager who knew how to act — F. W. P. Wyndham. If this did not betoken an immediate change in artistic policy, it did mean a radical shift in management structure. The ultimate effect of this was to create a theatrical empire, but, as far as the immediate future of the Lyceum was concerned, the new situation was possibly more important. When the challenge of 1914 came along, the theatre was more than ready to cope with it.

Saints and Sinners: A typical touring production, pre-1914. Henry Arthur Jones, probably the most skilful dramatist of his day, made his name with melodrama before turning to comedy.

ROYAL LYCEUM THEATRE.

Mr Thomas Thornes Company in

Saints & Sinners

WRITTEN BY

Mr HENRY A. JONES

JOINT AUTHOR OF THE
SILVER KING

PRODUCED BY

Mr THOMAS THORNE

Monday, May 25—SIX NIGHTS ONLY.

3   Enter the impresario

> Wyndham seems to be a rude boor.
> Though his father and mine were old
> friends and he was in the theatre every
> night, he never came near me. Quite unlike
> poor old Howard, a rough but good fellow
> — dead now as many good fellows have
> been, before they could be spared.

These words were written by H. B. Irving, son of the famous Sir Henry, on the occasion of his appearance as Hamlet with the Philip Ben Greet Company at the Lyceum in 1896. Whether or not Wyndham was quite as ill-mannered as 'Young Harry' suggests — and since Wyndham was in dispute with Irving's manager, Ben Greet, at the time, his avoidance of the young actor might well have been diplomatic rather than discourteous — need not really concern us here. The key phrase in that passage is 'quite unlike poor old Howard'. In many important respects, Wyndham was indeed a very different man from his old partner and, under his sole management, the Lyceum gradually became a very different kind of theatre.

It is quite impossible to tell, of course, what might have happened had Howard lived. It could, indeed, be argued that the subtle, but quite perceptible, changes in policy which took place between 1895 and 1914 would have gone ahead irrespective of his death. One suspects not, however — if only because this shift in policy, to begin with at least, was a matter of style rather than content. Howard had been fundamentally an actor, a showman, an artist: Wyndham was essentially a manager, a businessman, an impresario.

On the face of it, the theatre carried on pretty much as it had done for the previous twelve years. This was still, after all, the era of the actor-manager and all the great ones continued to play the Lyceum. Before his death in 1905, Sir Henry Irving was a regular visitor, playing the Lyceum

**Dame Marie Tempest:
A glamourous actress
as well as a fine
singer, Marie Tempest
appeared at the
Lyceum in many of
George Edwarde's
shows. Her long
career began in opera
and ended in light
comedy.**

another five times, four of which were with Ellen Terry, the fifth (and last) with her sister, Marion, in 1904. In the February of that same year, Ellen Terry brought her own company to the Lyceum for the last time.

On Irving's death, his position as undisputed leader of the English theatre was taken over by the great Sir Herbert Beerbohm Tree, whose lavish productions of Shakespeare (not to mention his creation of the role of Svengali in George du Maurier's *Trilby*) created a legend which is still very much alive today. Tree had little connection with Edinburgh and his appearances at the Lyceum, though frequent and invariably successful, never quite managed to generate that particular brand of excitement of which Irving had been capable. As far as Edinburgh was concerned, Irving's mantle fell on the shoulders of an actor-manager of quite a different stamp — the comedian Edward Compton.

The immense affection in which Compton was held in Edinburgh may have had something to do with the fact that he had strong Scottish connections — he was the grandson of a Scottish manse — but, whatever the reason for it, it was an affection which Compton both enjoyed and reciprocated. 'You'll have a critical audience there,' he remarked to his son, Montague Compton, on the occasion of the premiere production of the latter's first play in 1907, 'the most critical audience in Great Britain. If Edinburgh audiences approve, you'll have nothing to worry about.'

That particular season proved, in fact, to be the most interesting of all Compton's visits to the Lyceum. Five plays were to be performed during the course of the week — *School for Scandal, The Rivals, She Stoops to Conquer*, Robertson's *David Garrick* and Montague Compton's *The Gentleman in Grey* — and Compton, of course, was to play the leading role in them all. On the journey from the previous week's engagement in Aberdeen, however, Compton caught a cold and lost his voice as a result. He obviously would be unable to open in Edinburgh and had been about to call up the understudies, but young Montague would not hear of it.

He himself had played the part of Surface in a school production of *School for Scandal* and was confident that he would be able to stand in for his father. Although there was no time for rehearsal, he did so with great success, carrying off the entire performance without the need for a single prompt, a feat of courage and skill which paved the way for the warm reception that his own play received at the end of the week. After the fall of the final curtain on the first performance of *The Gentleman in Grey*, Compton (who had, by this time, completely recovered from his cold) led his son out to a cheering, enthusiastic audience. 'Was the play a success?' he called out to them. The reply was both instantaneous and unanimous — 'Yes!'

Montague Compton, however, was not convinced. Although *The Gentleman in Grey* initiated a long and prolific literary career, the young writer was disappointed with the stage and turned away from it to concentrate on novels and essays. In the course of his career, Montague reclaimed the family name (which was really Mackenzie, Compton being a stage name), gained the knighthood that his father had been denied, and, in the last years, made a home in the city where he had scored his first success. In the years before his death in 1972, there were few better-known figures among the Edinburgh citizenry than Sir Compton Mackenzie.

As for his father, Edward Compton continued to visit Edinburgh regularly for the rest of his acting career. His popularity never diminished and, on one occasion, his arrival in the city was greeted by the publication in the local paper of a seven-stanza poem, of which the following is the beginning:

> Thanks, Compton very much indeed
> For kindly gracing thus our city, mate.
> We're always glad to have a feed
> From *menu* old — the true legitimate.

The 'true legitimate' apart, however, important changes are quite discernible in these opening years of the new century. The most significant of these affected the work of the resident company. Under Howard, of course, this had been an important part of the Lyceum's activities,

Sir Compton Mackenzie: Sir Compton first came to Edinburgh in 1907, when his play, 'The Gentleman in Grey' was performed at the Lyceum by his father's company. Towards the end of his life, he made the city his home.

playing mainly in the summer months to visiting tourists. Although they performed many English and Irish plays, the company were particularly strong in the field of Scottish drama, in which Howard had an abiding interest. In the last twelve years of his life, Howard not only produced new versions of *Rob Roy, The Lady of the Lake, The Heart of Midlothian, Kenilworth* and *Old Mortality*, he also commissioned a stage version of *Marmion* from the novelist and playwright Robert Buchanan. If such plays were not produced at the Lyceum, it was clear that they would seldom be produced elsewhere. After Howard's death, however, this strand of Lyceum policy was abandoned and, apart from pantomimes, there were no resident productions for the next three decades. A touring production of *The Bride of Lammermoor* in 1908 (under the management of Sir John Martin Harvey, who also played Ravenswood) was the last Scottish play of any kind to be seen in the theatre for many years thereafter.

At the same time, a completely different and, at that time, very new form of theatre began to appear on the Lyceum stage. Towards the end of 1895, the George Edwardes Company from Daly's Theatre in London appeared in a play called *Don Juan* by J. L. Tomer. Billed as 'burlesque' it was, in fact, something rather different. George Edwardes was an Irishman who had began his career in theatre management at the Gaiety Theatre in Dublin. John Hollingshead of the London Gaiety had brought him to London, first as a partner, then to succeed Hollingshead when he retired. In 1891, Edwardes had built Daly's Theatre for Augustin Daly and in the course of the next forty years became something of an institution in British theatrical life. Known throughout his career by the soubriquet 'The Guvnor', Edwardes' approach to the theatre is best summed up in some words of his predecessor. Writing of the casting policy at the old Gaiety, 'Practical John' Hollingshead declared:

> The choice of the ladies on the stage, except for a few chosen singers where voice was an object, was openly and avowedly governed by a desire to put pleasing forms and faces before the public. My view of the stage was,

whatever it might be, judged from the lofty, not to say stuck-up heights of literature and art, it was not a platform for the display of grandmothers and maiden aunts. If physical beauty could be got in connection with brains and dramatic talent, so much the better, but my first duty seemed to me to get physical beauty and I got it.

These words describe the theatrical approach which gave rise to the phrase 'Gaiety Girl'. George Edwardes shared this approach but added several other elements; the firm plot-lines of straight drama and the music of light opera. The result became known as musical comedy.

More than any other single manager, George Edwardes was responsible for the creation of musical comedy as a theatrical form. His management, which lasted right up until the end of the nineteen-twenties was responsible for literally dozens of West End hits. Indeed, some of his shows — the English version of *The Merry Widow*, for instance, and *The Maid of the Mountains* — retain a measure of popularity even today. In addition to this, he was a star-maker, casting a girl in the chorus and building her up until she became a household name. His most famous star, however, did not begin in this way. She was the most glamorous woman ever to appear on a stage anywhere in the world and her name was Marie Tempest.

Marie Tempest, later Dame Marie Tempest, seems to have been aptly named. By all accounts, anyone who had anything to do with her was in for a stormy passage. She had a most varied career, beginning in 1891 as a singer in a production of *Carmen* and ended it in the late 'thirties in Dodie Smith's *Dear Octopus*. Part of her transition between opera and straight drama was made via musical comedy and she was with George Edwardes for five years, playing leading roles throughout this time. The shows in which she appeared were among the most successful that Edwardes ever had: she was Adele in *An Artist's Model*, O Mimosa San in *The Geisha* and Maia in *A Greek Slave*, appearing at the Lyceum in all of these roles. Edwardes treated her like royalty, always making sure that there was a carriage waiting for her outside the stage door to whisk her away after each performance. Nevertheless, when Marie Tempest left the company in 1900, she did so in a rather characteristic manner.

It came about as the result of a show called *San Toy*, in which she played the title role. At one point in the play, Edwardes wanted her to appear in a man's long trousers, a piece of costuming which would have been sensational in 1900. Marie, however, refused on the grounds that such an appearance would constitute a lapse of taste and would be seen as such by the audience. When Edwardes insisted, Marie defied him and cut the trousers down into shorts, making, one imagines, an even more sensational appearance in the amended costume. Sensational or not, however, Edwardes was furious and presented Marie with an ultimatum. She could either use the costumes provided or leave the company. Marie Tempest left and never worked in musical comedy again.

If Marie Tempest thought that her departure would have a serious effect on Edwardes' business, she was mistaken. He was much too astute a manager to put all his eggs in one basket. His company's association with the Lyceum, for instance, became very close and for a number of years the Edinburgh theatre was almost a second home to him. Far from being just another touring production that was appearing at the theatre, an Edwardes show would often be the exact opposite. Frequently, Edwardes would run in a new show at the Lyceum, trying it out prior to its opening at Daly's. The Lyceum, therefore, can be seen to have played a rather significant part in the beginnings of musical comedy.

It was Wyndham, of course, who brought Edwardes to the Lyceum and encouraged him to develop an audience for musical comedy in Edinburgh. At the same time, a more serious (although less popular) form of musical theatre was not neglected. Opera continued to feature prominently at the Lyceum, with seasons from the D'Oyly Carte, Carl Rosa and Moody-Manners Companies. One of the more interesting aspects of the activities of these companies was a certain interest in the fostering of new work by native composers. The Moody-Manners Company was particularly enthusiastic about this, awarding a series of prizes for new operas in English by British composers. Formed by the bass Charles Manners and his wife Fanny Moody in 1898, the Moody-Manners Company was at one time the largest and most successful touring opera company in the country. Indeed, they were actually two companies — one of 175 singers and musicians another, much smaller, of 95 singers and musicians — and when their activities came to an end in 1916, they left a big gap in British theatrical life. They did a great deal to extend the repertoire of English opera.

From a Scottish point of view, however, it was the Royal Carl Rosa Opera Company who made the greatest contribution. At the Lyceum in 1894, they premiered *Jeanie Deans,* a new opera by Hamish McCunn (who was, incidentally, the head conductor of the Moody-Manners Company) and they also commissioned work from another two Scottish composers, Alexander Campbell Mackenzie and Alick Maclean. The Royal Carl Rosa Company continued to play the Lyceum right up until almost the end of the 'twenties.

What with serious drama, musical comedy from Edwardes, the opera seasons and the continuing pantomime tradition, it can be seen that the spirit of eclecticism continued to be pursued at the Lyceum, notwithstanding the loss of the resident company. It was in the field of theatre administration, however, that the greatest changes took place in the years leading up to the First World War. Very largely, these were dictated by the formation and growth of the firm of Howard & Wyndham Ltd.

As was mentioned in the previous chapter, this limited company was established in 1895, shortly before Howard's death, based on the following four theatres: the Royal Lyceum, Edinburgh, the Theatre Royal, Edinburgh, the Theatre Royal, Glasgow, the Royalty Theatre, Glasgow.

Of these four, the Edinburgh theatres and the Glasgow Theatre Royal were wholly owned by the company, while the Glasgow Royalty had been taken under lease. In 1896, the company took a lease on another theatre, the Tyne in Newcastle-on-Tyne, and around the turn of the century they began acquiring property in Edinburgh and Glasgow, including some storage space in the West Port, Edinburgh. In 1904, the company acquired another Glasgow theatre — the King's — but as far as the history of the Lyceum is concerned, the next significant transaction took place in 1906.

In that year, an Edinburgh builder called Cruikshank found himself in something of a spot. He had just completed the construction of a very large theatre in Leven Street, but the company that had placed the contract had gone bankrupt. A deal was made with Howard & Wyndham Ltd., as a result of which the builder's son, A. Stewart Cruikshank, joined the board of the company and Edinburgh had a new theatre — the King's.

Stewart Cruikshank was very young at this time and had had no experience whatsoever of theatre management. He worked very hard at learning the business, however, and five years later was appointed director of the King's, the theatre with which he was to be identified for the rest of his life. In time, he would not only become both chairman and managing director of Howard & Wyndham Ltd., but would hand over the succession to his son.

The acquisition of the King's was to have a serious influence on the Lyceum in the years to come. Since Howard & Wyndham Ltd. now owned three Edinburgh theatres, there was obviously no sense in running them in direct competition with each other. Over the years, a co-ordinated policy evolved which led in time to each of the theatres developing their own, distinct identity in the minds of the Edinburgh public. The Theatre Royal became closely identified with the Scottish music hall tradition, while the King's earned a considerable reputation for pantomime and big, lavish musicals. The Lyceum, in a modern phrase, became the most 'up-market' of the three, specialising in straight drama, opera and the more sophisticated forms of light entertainment.

All of this was very much in the

future, however. At the time, Wyndham and his colleagues were content to leave this evolving policy to take care of itself and to concentrate on consolidating the growth of the company. In 1909, an actor called George T. Minshull joined the company as joint managing director, possibly to fill the role that had been vacated by Howard's death fourteen years earlier, and to allow Wyndham more time to develop the business side of the growing venture. In 1912, Wyndham made what was possibly his greatest coup, taking over the Robert Arthur group of six theatres. This meant that the number of theatres under Howard & Wyndham control was raised from four to ten. No fewer than five of these theatres were in England: apart from the Tyne theatre, held under lease, the company owned another theatre in Newcastle, two in Liverpool (the Shakespeare and the Royal Court) and another in Nottingham. Additionally, Howard & Wyndham not only had a presence in Edinburgh and Glasgow, but also in Dundee and Aberdeen. In less than twenty years, therefore, the company had not only doubled in size, but had extended its sphere of influence greatly throughout the United Kingdom. At the outbreak of war in 1914, Howard & Wyndham Ltd. were more than capable of meeting the challenge that it presented.

The First World War, of course had a cataclysmic effect on all sections of British society. For four years and three months, the fact of war was all-pervasive, impregnating every nook and cranny of British life and changing it entirely. Gold sovereigns gave way to bank-notes, inflation roared and Government restrictions entered the lives of the people to a greater extent than ever before. Worst of all, young men from every walk of life found themselves thrust into uniform and sent off to the front, either to die in their thousands or to return changed men, disillusioned and altered irreversibly by the experience. There was a loss of innocence during the First World War that did more permanent damage to the quality of life than any of the Kaiser's bombs.

In the theatre, the effect of the war was double-edged. As far as business was

61

concerned, the war created a boom as people sought escape from the realities of the conflict. As audience levels reached unprecedented heights, however, it soon became apparent that it was not the theatre of Irving and Tree that was wanted — there was little escape to be found in Shakespeare or any other serious dramatist — and so poetry, mystery and quality drama was forced to surrender the stage to music, colour and pretty young girls. The theatrical philosophy of 'Practical John' Hollingshead came into its own with a vengeance. Burlesque, revue and musical comedy were all the rage.

Speculators with no real interest in the theatre discovered that there was money to be made in this and, as a result, theatre rentals shot up in price. An average rent in 1914, for instance, would be something of the order of £25 — two years later, this had gone up to £500. The speculators, whose motives were confined to a straightforward return on capital, could afford to accommodate this extra cost while keeping seat-prices stable — but the actor-managers could not. They had always operated on a very narrow margin and, with the coming of the war, most of them simply went out of business. The actor-manager circuit, the backbone of the British theatre for decades, simply collapsed. It was the end of an era.

A few brave spirits managed to soldier on into the 'twenties. Perhaps the most lovably eccentric of those who managed to do so was one of the Lyceum's most regular visitors, Sir Frank Benson. Benson, who was knighted on the stage at Drury Lane during the Shakespeare Tercentenary in 1916, founded the Stratford Festival and probably did more than any other actor, before or since, to popularise Shakespeare's drama. His management began in the eighteen-eighties and lasted until the early nineteen-thirties and at one time he had no fewer than four companies on the road. Of his acting, the critic James Agate wrote:

> About Benson in his heyday I cannot, and
> will not, be dispassionate. He gave what, to
> a young playgoer, seemed tremendous
> things. The thwarted walk of Hamlet; the
> blood-encrusted, wholly barbaric Macbeth;

the patrician in Coriolanus; the zoological, unsentimentalised Caliban. . . . He had four things most modern actors lack — presence, a profile befitting a Roman coin, voice, and virility to make you believe that Orlando overthrew more than his enemies.

Hesketh Pearson, while largely endorsing Agate's view, suggests that Benson's popularity with schoolboy audiences had a great deal to do with the spectacular athleticism of the fight scenes he staged. Benson certainly seems to have been a very athletic man, interested as much in sport as he was in drama, a fact that is illustrated by the way in which Oscar Ashe, one of the many fine actors to emerge from Benson's company, was given his first opportunity in the theatre. Ashe was an Australian and played a more than competent game of cricket. When he came to Britain, he had enormous difficulty in getting a start in the theatre, finally being hired by the Benson company, so the story goes, because Benson had a desperate need for a wicket-keeper at the time!

By the time Benson was knighted in 1916 (the only time, incidentally, that an actor has received his knighthood within the actual precincts of a theatre) he was one of a dying breed. It should not be supposed, however, that the actor-managers were replaced by personalities who were any duller or less colourful. If anything, the opposite was true. The independent producers who came into their own during the First World War may have been a very different breed with a different style, but they were every bit as vital and individual in character.

For instance, there was the enigmatic George Dance, later knighted for his philanthropy. Dance, who first brought a company to the Lyceum in 1905 with Messager's opera *Veronique*, amassed a huge fortune out of touring, a great deal of which he simply gave away. A self-confessed philistine, Dance had started off as a librettist and book-writer for pantomime and never had the slightest interest in serious drama. In spite of this, when the Old Vic Company very nearly went out of existence through lack of funds in the late 'twenties, it was Dance who came to the rescue with a cheque for £30,000. According to W. MacQueen Pope, who worked for Dance for a time and could testify both to his generosity and his philistinism, no explanation was ever forthcoming for this munificent act. On another occasion, Dance sent MacQueen Pope down to Salisbury to see if it would be possible to buy Stonehenge. Not surprisingly, 'Popie' found that Stonehenge was not for sale — but one wonders, if it had been, what Dance would have done with it!

Another producer of musical comedy — and one who was given a special welcome in Edinburgh — was Robert Courtneidge. A poor boy from the Abbeyhill district of the city, Courtneidge's career actually began at the Lyceum, where he worked as a call-boy. Encouraged by Howard to go on the stage and following the Scottish tradition of the lad-o-pairts, Courtneidge worked hard to educate himself, succeeding to such an extent that his son-in-law, a Cambridge graduate, was to describe him in later life as 'just like one of the dons at Caius'. After spending some time acting and directing in Australia, Courtneidge returned to Britain and for some years was in charge of productions at two Manchester theatres, the Prince's and the Royal. A fine director, he won particular acclaim for his production of *A Midsummer Night's Dream* and was persuaded, because of this, to try his luck in London. For a brief period he worked with the George Edwardes management, and it was during this time that he first returned to Edinburgh with his own production of *The Duchess of Dantzic.*

Edwardes was most impressed by Courtneidge and offered him a partnership at Daly's. Courtneidge, however, was shrewd enough to realise that he had a future of his own and declined. Throughout the war years, his was one of the most popular companies to occupy the Lyceum, appearing in the theatre more frequently than any other, with the exception of Edwardes himself. That this fine director should have been forced to turn from Shakespeare to musical comedy is a fact which tells us a great deal about the theatrical atmosphere of the time. Apart from his greatest success, *The Arcadians* (1909), most of the shows he produced are forgotten now, but there is one other, at least, which retains a certain interest. This was a musical play called *Young England*, which Courtneidge brought to the Lyceum in 1915. It featured a light comedian called Jack Hulbert. Approximately a year later, in 1916, Hulbert married Courtneidge's youngest daughter Cicely, thus beginning one of the longest-running and best-loved stage partnerships the theatre has ever known.

Edwardes, Courtneidge, Dance and others ensured that the Lyceum kept its audience at a time when the theatre was undergoing a radical change. At the same time, the growth in power and influence of Howard & Wyndham Ltd. protected the Lyceum from the financial snowstorm which, in spite of the boom, was causing many theatres to close down. Even after the introduction of Entertainment Tax in 1916, seat prices were maintained at more or less pre-war levels — ranging from 10/6 for stalls and dress circle to 1/- for the gallery — and margins were extremely tight. Smaller organisations just could not stand the pace and those that were not taken over by the larger groups were usually bought up for a song by men whose only interest was bricks and mortar.

Both as an impresario and a businessman, therefore, Wyndham brought the Lyceum through a difficult time. With all his instincts and abilities, however, even he could not protect the theatre from the sweeping social changes which permanently affected the life of the community. The great upheaval which took place in British society during the First World War was as evident in Edinburgh as it was anywhere else and created a change in the status of the Lyceum which was to last for more than a decade.

Part of this change, of course, was created by outside influences. Chief among these was the emergence of the cinema as a form of popular entertainment. Although it was not yet the threat it was to become when sound was introduced, the cinema did make a significant impact on both the customs and the attitudes of theatre audiences. The conventions regarding dress, for instance, were largely abandoned because the cinema did not insist on them. At the same time, the cinema, even the early silent cinema, was able to produce effects and show the audience sights that the live theatre could not possibly match. The earthquake scene in *Claudian* might have seemed ineffective in 1884, but it would have been laughable in 1918.

The cinema was also largely responsible for extending the American influence which had begun to take effect at that time. Among the great number of British men and women who had been caught up by the war was a large segment of the entertainment industry. This gap was filled by the influx of American entertainers, giving British audiences their first thrilling contact with American show business. When America finally entered the war, American troops began to arrive and the interest in all things American gathered momentum. Jazz music was discovered and led to a great craze for dancing. The American form of musical comedy, which had had a parallel development to the British variety, gave an added impetus to a form of theatre that was already very popular.

All of this had a serious effect on public taste, but the most radical change of all had been created, not by any external development but by the effect of the war on the perceptions of the average member of the audience. Theatre exists always on its ability to create wonder in the hearts and minds of the audience and, as has already been mentioned, there was a loss of innocence during the First World War which altered this capacity completely and forever. It has often been suggested that, if post-war audiences had been able to see him, they would not have found Sir Henry Irving in the least credible. Although this is questionable — ignoring, as it does, the ability of a great actor to relate to his audience — one can understand the logic of the argument. After all that had happened during the most bloody four years in recent history, the conscience of Matthias in *The Bells* probably would have seemed more than a little overstated.

Since Irving had died in 1905, this argument cannot be other than speculative, but there is no doubt at all about another great innovator of the nineteenth century. In 1919, a producer called Eade Montefiore attempted, with a singular lack of success, to revive the plays of T. W. Robertson. Robertson's comedies, so popular and, indeed, revolutionary in their time, were considered trivial by audiences who had become accustomed to the music, glamour and 'smart' humour of Courtneidge and Edwardes.

The change, however, was more than a change in taste — it was a change in the way that change itself was made. Control of the theatre had passed from the hands of dedicated, professional actors into the grasp of tough-minded, commercial managers who, although they had their own standards of excellence, would always put profit before any artistic ideal. The immediate effect was to create a theatre in which the standards of the lowest common denominator were paramount. Although no theatre management — then, now, or ever — can afford to ignore the perceptions of its audience, the fact remains that, prior to 1914, standards were set by the theatre: for more than a decade after 1918, these standards were set largely by the audience.

For the Lyceum, the consequences of this new situation were dire indeed, leading to what was possibly the bleakest period in the theatre's entire history. In the early days, Howard had invested the theatre with a degree of individuality and style, running the theatre in the classic manner of the actor-manager, evolving a house style, acting in it whenever he could, living for the theatre, sometimes, indeed, even living *in* the theatre. Even after Howard's death, Wyndham had been able to maintain this individuality, albeit in a slightly different manner. Immediately after the First World War, however, the concept of such a distinctive character had, perforce, to go by the board. The audience wanted the 'latest thing' and, such was the climate of the times that the Lyceum management had no choice but to accede to the demand of the audience, make sure that the 'latest thing' was available.

And the 'latest thing' in those days, came only from London.

4 West End, Edinburgh

The term 'West End', automatically associated all over the world with the glittering lights of the London theatre, has another, quite different connotation in Edinburgh, where it exists as a geographical, as well as an abstract expression. The small but extremely prosperous area around the West End of Princes Street was once considered so smart that poorer people would enter it only with a degree of hesitation. One of the few reasons that they would have had for doing so would have been to visit the Lyceum, which has always been acutely aware of its identification with the part of the city in which it is located. Throughout the Lyceum's history there has been a feeling (which persists, to some extent, even today) that a theatre that is situated in the West End of Edinburgh ought to maintain standards that are as superior as its surroundings. Although, as we shall see, this has brought the Lyceum problems as well as advantages, the most important effect of this state of affairs has been to ensure that the theatre has constantly been under pressure to pursue a unique and distinctive style of its own. This, in turn, has given the Lyceum a sense of identity and purpose that has endured for decades.

The only period in which the Lyceum was in any danger of losing this sense of identity was during the nineteen-twenties, when the conditions which prevailed in the British theatre worked against such individuality and very nearly turned the theatre into just another anonymous provincial playhouse. It was at this time that the changed situation described in the previous chapter really began to take effect, bringing with it a completely new attitude towards the whole business of theatre.

In the pre-war period, theatre management had been professional rather than commercial — i.e. the old actor-managers had aimed at

Dame Gladys Cooper: An actress whose beauty, style and talent had a special appeal for Edinburgh audiences of the twenties and thirties.

69

making a reasonable profit after clearing their costs. As far as the new impresarios were concerned, however, this simply was not good enough. They were gamblers by instinct who spent a lot of money in order to make the largest possible profit. When they had a successful London production they would seek to maximise this profit by putting as many as four separate touring companies around the country. Although the advertising for these companies often gave the impression that they would be performing the original London production, this was rarely true, particularly as the decade wore on. This tends to detract from the interest that many of the productions might otherwise have possessed, as a brief examination of some of them will show.

In 1920, a musical play by Jerome Kern, *Sally*, was one of the hits of the year. When it opened in London at the Winter Garden, a young American actress created a sensation in the title role. Her name was Dorothy Dickson and she was so pretty that the audience literally gasped in wonder when she made her first entrance. When the play came to Edinburgh, the part was played by an actress called Margaret Campbell and, whether or not audiences gasped at *her* first entrance, nobody saw fit to report it.

In 1923, José Collins and Bertram Wallis appeared in the hugely successful *Catherine* (based on the life of Catherine the Great of Russia) at the London Gaiety. In this lavish production, Jose Collins wore a wedding dress that was made entirely out of sequins and which was so heavy that it took three people to carry it. They did not carry it all the way to Edinburgh, however, nor did the stars of the show appear at the Lyceum. Their parts were played in Edinburgh by Sylvia Cecil and Caspar Middleton.

In 1926, the controversial drama critic Hannan Swaffer made a vicious attack on a play called *The Green Hat*, by Michael Arlen. When the play was performed at the Lyceum, it received a somewhat cooler reception, possibly because its theme, the Mayfair smart set, did not mean much in Scotland's capital city. At the same time, the fact that the leading actress, Tallulah Bankhead, did not appear at the Lyceum may have had something to do with it. Miss Bankhead's part was taken over by Phyllis Thomas.

Finally, in 1925, the musical *No, No, Nanette* took London by storm, becoming a classic of its kind. The original production starred Binnie Hale, George Grossmith and Joseph Coyne, replaced at the Lyceum by Cora Griffin, Arthur Riscoe and Charles Heslop. By this time, the pattern had been established: a London success was kept running, while duplicate companies were sent to tour the provinces.

The main effect of this new policy was to create a rift between London and the provinces that had never existed before. London, of course, has always been the centre of the British theatre, but that did not mean that the provinces were despised or considered in the least second-rate. Sir Henry Irving, for example, would have been appalled at the suggestion that he should send a replacement on tour while he continued to play in London. In those days, of course, the audience came to see the actor rather than the play and Irving and the others would never have been able to pursue such a policy effectively. The theatre had changed completely and it was only in the new conditions that such a policy was possible. In carrying it out, the men who ran the theatre did not intend to slight the provinces, but were simply concerned to achieve the highest possible return on capital. The effect, however, remained the same. During the nineteen-twenties, the British theatre lost a unity that it has never since recovered. It was at this time that the term 'provincial tour' took on a suggestion of something grossly inferior to 'West End production'.

Edinburgh is not a provincial city and the Lyceum has never been content to consider itself a provincial playhouse. Edinburgh's West End (particularly the West End of those days) does not take kindly to being offered anything less than the best that the theatre has to offer. If London did not realise this, the directors of Howard & Wyndham Ltd. certainly did. Although they understood, and to some extent had helped to create, the new system of touring, they realised that there was a limit to which this system could be applied at the Lyceum. Although he was now in his last years, Wyndham was still very active and he had certainly not forgotten the pledge that he and Howard had made back in 1883 — to make the Lyceum 'another name for what is best'. Several productions of the period show quite clearly that this intention remained a priority with the management.

From a purely historical point of view, the most important of these was the visit, in December 1923, of the Scottish National Players. This company (whose significance within the context of the history of Scottish theatre will be discussed in a later chapter) had been formed two years previously by the St Andrew Society of Glasgow with the specific intention of helping to create a native Scottish drama. Although this was very early in the history of the company — who were known, in the days before the formation of the Scottish National Party, as the S.N.P. — they had already gone some way towards justifying their 'national' title by virtue of the fact that they had recently been invited to play before King George V and Queen Mary at Balmoral. During their week at the Lyceum, the S.N.P. performed John Brandane's Highland comedy *The Glen is Mine*, preceded by (on different nights) Gordon Bottomley's *Gruach* (a one-act verse-drama on the theme of Shakespeare's *Macbeth*) and *Cute McCheyne*, an adaptation by A. P. Wilson of the short story by Joseph Laing Waugh.

These plays constitute the first indigenous drama to be seen on the Lyceum stage since the death of Howard, almost twenty years earlier. Taken together with the fact that all three plays were by contemporary Scottish authors, this may appear to suggest that the season would hold a special appeal to the Edinburgh public. The S.N.P. certainly seemed to think so. Their magazine, *The Scottish Player*, carried a publicity article which described the appeal they were trying to make.

> Perhaps this will be the first occasion when you really became conscious of the fact that there is in these days a stirring amongst the dead bones of our Scottish literature and

thought. We have much to do to make the
Renaissance as inspiring as that which set
the souls of many other nations aglow. We
can do what Ireland, Norway and Bohemia
have done; and your presence at the
performances advertized here will be a
contribution towards that work.

Edinburgh, unfortunately, did not
respond. The first night audience was extremely
thin and, despite excellent reviews, the situation did
not improve much during the course of the week.
This indifference may be explained partly by the
fact that the S.N.P. had been founded in Glasgow,
and apart from the fact that rivalry between the two
cities has always been fierce, Edinburgh might well
have resented the usurpation of its capital status
which is implicit in the 'national' title. In this
respect, it is interesting that *The Scotsman*, in an
otherwise encouraging review of *The Glen is Mine*,
made a statement that was to be echoed with
increasing strength, in later decades.

The audience seemed to care for this play
better than they did for 'Gruach' and,
though the wit is a trifle heavy at times,
there is a good deal of amusement to be
drawn from it. At the same time, there is
little distinction or beauty about the
comedy set beside a dialect play like 'Nan'
or 'Playboy of the Western World'. Drama
may be a reflection of life — and as a
reflection of character, the play is faithful
enough — but it should be a reflection seen
in the mirror of imagination. *One has the
right to expect this from a movement such as
the National Theatre Society.*

Whatever the Edinburgh public may
have felt — then, now, or hereafter — about the
term 'national theatre', it seems probable that their
disappointing response to the Scottish National
Players was based on rather more mundane
considerations. If they did not take kindly to second-
rate versions of London shows, they at least knew
that these were *professional* second-rate versions.
Whatever excellent qualities they may have
possessed, the S.N.P. were an *amateur* company, and
it is more than likely that the Edinburgh public was
not prepared to pay professional prices to see an
amateur show. It should be remembered, too, that

this was a period in which straight drama was in decline — not only at the Lyceum, but elsewhere in the British theatre — and the shows which had the greatest audience potential were those which had music, spectacle and glamour.

One such show was *Frasquita*, a new musical comedy with music by Franz Lehar, book by Fred de Gresac and lyrics by Reginald Arkell, premiered at the Lyceum under the management of George Edwardes at Christmas, 1924. The link between the Lyceum and the Edwardes management was now well into its third decade and although 'The Guvnor' often put touring productions into the theatre — one of the most notable being Frederick Lonsdale's *Madame Pompadour*, with Edith Cecil in the part created in London by Evelyn Laye — he still found it useful to 'run in' an occasional show prior to opening in London. *Frasquita* is a particularly good example of the typical Edwardes show of this period — even though, as things turned out, a triumphant success in Edinburgh was followed by a disastrous failure in London, where the show ran for only eighteen performances.

The story of *Frasquita* is a version of the story of *Carmen*, with a happy ending included to suit the musical comedy audience. A young man is smitten with love for a gypsy girl and runs away with her, only to find that she has lost interest in him. She returns to her gypsy lover, he to his fiancée and that, apart from a bit of dramatic tension in the way of a duel between the young man and the gypsy lover, is about all there is to it. As with all Edwardes' productions, everything was in the music, the lyrics, the costumes, the lighting — and, most of all, the cast.

The part of Frasquita was played by José Collins, the original *Maid of the Mountains* and undisputed Queen of Musical Comedy at that time. The illegitimate daughter of Lottie Collins, a music hall singer (whose main claim to fame was her popularising the song 'Tarara-boom-de-ay'), José Collins starred in a great many Edwardes shows, both at Daly's and the Gaiety. She first appeared at the Lyceum in 1920, in a show called *The Last*

Waltz, which later became the first musical ever to be broadcast live from a theatre. Bertam Wallis, José's usual partner, also appeared in *Frasquita* but possibly the most interesting member of the cast was a character actor who was later to make a successful career in Hollywood, Edmund Gwenn. In *Frasquita*, he played the part of Hippolyte Gallipot, a professor of anthropology whose particular area of study is the female of the species. His performance, which included a drag scene in which he impersonated a Spanish maid, was one of the high points of the show.

In 1923, Fred Astaire and his sister Adele made their first tour of the British Isles in a musical farce called *Stop Flirting!*. Their exciting and, at that time, innovative style of dancing took audiences everywhere by storm and they repeated the tour the following year. They were, therefore, seen at the Lyceum twice, and *The Scotsman* review of their second appearance is quoted in full.

> *Stop Flirting!* returns to the Lyceum with the stamp of success upon it. The favourable impressions formed of this breezy musical farce less than a year ago found their reflection last night, for the theatre was crowded in every part and the players received with enthusiasm. It well repays a second visit, less for its merits as a farce than for the ability of a company whose work raises it above the common place. Conventional devices in the construction of the story are skilfully glossed over. The main theme of the adventure of the young man whose fiancée is prone to flirtation is at times not stressed; the incidentals then matter and they are always entertaining. The dancing of Adele and Fred Astaire, for example, is something of which the audience cannot get enough. They are distinctive exponents of their art. There was genuine humour in the clever dance which followed the singing of 'The Whichness of the Whatness' towards the end of the second act, and, smiling and obliging, the couple responded to five or six enthusiastic recalls. The standard they set is maintained by the others. Dorothy Waring sings and acts well as the fiancée who thinks that a little flirting will help her to

keep the affections of Perry Reynolds, and Mimi Crawford plays a rather difficult part with marked cleverness, her dancing being particularly attractive. The role of the troubled young lover is taken by Jack Melford, who shows a sure touch for light comedy. Ably backed up by E. Louis Bradfield, he extracts much fun from situations which might easily fall flat. George de Warfax also contributes to the humour of the piece as an Italian guest. The other parts are ably filled, and a capable chorus help the farce along to success.

Scotsman reviewers, in those days, were both anonymous and required to maintain a large degree of objectivity in their coverage, a fact which may, in part, account for a certain defensive coolness in the above review. It is just possible, however, to discern a note of hostility lying beneath the surface of the reviewer's praise. Certainly, one would never guess, from such a review, the extent of the sensation that had been created by the appearance of the Astaires. This note of hostility was to sound stronger the following year, when another great star of musical comedy appeared at the Lyceum.

Jack Buchanan was one of the most successful and popular of all Scottish entertainers. Born in Helensburgh in 1891, he first appeared in London in 1912 and, in the space of ten years, worked his way to the very top of his profession. A debonair song-and-dance man, a fine comedy actor, an accomplished director and a more than capable manager, Jack Buchanan brought to every department of his activities a degree of charm, style and wit, the like of which has been seldom seen since. He went to America, where he had equal success as the very prototype of the English man-about-town. He made a number of films and, although it is now considered that his talent never quite made the step from stage to screen, he had a success in this medium as recently as 1953 in *The Band Wagon*, in which he starred, coincidentally enough, with Fred Astaire. Late in his career, he had some success in the new medium of television, which had been invented by his boyhood friend,

John Logie Baird. In a phrase of the invaluable W. MacQueen Pope, Jack Buchanan was 'really West End'. In spite of this, however, he remained resolutely Scottish, his Scottishness being of a kind that few Englishmen (and no Americans) can understand.

Jack Buchanan could not possibly fail at the Lyceum — and he didn't. The occasion was February 1925 and Buchanan and his company had just returned from America, where they had considerable success with a show called *Boodle*. Besides Buchanan himself, the cast included a comedienne called Veronica Brady and an attractive young soubrette known simply as June. June (full name June Howard-Tripp) was to have a remarkable career over the next forty years. Starting off in the 'twenties, she was basically a dancer who became a comedienne, but at the end of the Second World War, she gave up dancing for a no less successful career as a journalist with Beaverbrook, finally writing (according to Vivian Ellis) 'a stage autobiography that actually wasn't ghosted'. Among other things, June became famous for being the girl in the song *I Danced with a Man (Who Danced with a Girl Who Danced with the Prince of Wales)*.

The combination of Jack Buchanan and June must have been glamorously irresistible. *The Scotsman*, while acknowledging the effectiveness of the performance, began its review of *Boodle* with the following paragraph:

'Boodle', presented last night at the Lyceum theatre for the first time in Edinburgh, prior to its presentation in London, is of the type of entertainment fittingly described as a 'show'. The programme defines it as a musical play, a term which covers a multitude of variations. It is largely farcical in character, yet not a farce, for that term implies some degree of continuity and adhesion to type. One can well imagine that its authors would care little about type so long as the thing 'goes'. A combination of assets served last night to make the piece 'go' without any degree of doubt. One of these is the appearance of Mr Jack Buchanan and the young artiste known as

June. Both fit admirably into a production in which the play is of little account, but where the incidental details and the manner of presentation are the things that matter. With their numerous associates, they manage to create an atmosphere of brightness and irresponsible gaiety, and, with an audience eager to be amused, the rest is easy.

The sneering tone of this paragraph seems rather puzzling in a review that is otherwise full of praise. It should be remembered, however, that in 1925 the Lyceum was still associated in many minds with the old pre-war theatre of Sir Henry Irving and the actor-managers. In those days, any production which displayed the slightest tendency to 'play to the gallery' was regarded as possessing a definite lack of distinction. Small wonder that people like the anonymous *Scotsman* reviewer should have regarded the dominance of musical comedy at the Lyceum with something akin to revulsion.

As the decade wore on, however, it became increasingly obvious that this dominance was not going to become a permanent feature at the Lyceum. After 1925, the preponderance of musical shows began to give way to more and more straight drama, although still performed, of course, by touring companies from London. Although the records are no longer available, it is probably fair to assume that a certain fall in the box-office revenue may have had something to do with this. Apart from the fact that audiences were getting tired of musicals — it was not possible, after all, to present artistes like Jack Buchanan and Fred Astaire every week — they are very expensive shows to stage, with a much greater risk factor, particularly when one remembers that the theatre was coming under increasing pressure from the new media of the cinema and sound broadcasting. Slowly, the spirit of eclecticism, the ruling principle of the original management, began to reassert itself.

It was not possible, of course, to go back to the old days of the actor-managers. Although there were a number of companies that were run by actors, these were not actor-managers in the old sense of the term — i.e. they did not operate from the base of a London theatre and they did not have financial control over their activities. However, there were a few who kept up the old style of presentation. These included Henry Baynton (often, however, with backing from Robert Courtneidge), Mathieson Lang (mentor of the last great actor-manager of them all, Donald Wolfit) and, as ever, there was Sir Frank Benson, with his company of athletic young actors whose stage fighting thrilled schoolboy audiences everywhere. Benson's company, however, contained much dramatic, as well as athletic talent, and in 1928, it included two young actors who would later, each in his own way, become household names.

In May 1926, the Bensonians presented *Hamlet* at the Lyceum, with Sir Frank in the part of the Ghost of Hamlet's Father and Arthur Phillips as the Prince. The part of Guildenstern was played by future film star Robert Donat, while a number of smaller parts were played by television's original 'Dr Who', William Hartnell. Among the rest of the cast were many names which would later grace the British stage in leading roles — including James Kirkham, Norman Claridge and Molly Sainton, who played Ophelia.

Straight drama, then, was beginning to make something of a comeback, after the years of musical and lightweight comedy. It was not always successful, of course, and it soon became clear that the romantic style of the Victorians would no longer succeed in its appeal. In 1928, Charles Doran's company made an attempt to revive Wilson Barrett's *The Sign of the Cross*, but it made little impact on an audience which was becoming increasingly less religious and which had, in any case, only recently seen the original screen version of *King of Kings*. The fact that Barrett's play was successfully filmed four years later would seem to confirm the view that, henceforth, such themes would be more effectively handled by the cinema.

The Lyceum management was, of course, well aware of the competition that the cinema was beginning to present at this time and had, in fact, attempted on at least two separate

79

occasions to present the new medium in the theatre. The first of these had been as early as 1912, when Charles Urban's 'Live Motion Pictures in Kinema-colour' had played the theatre for three weeks. This had been a charity season in which all of the proceeds were handed over to the fund for the widows and orphans of those who had perished in the *Titanic* disaster. The second occasion, in 1924, was a presentation by Ideal Films Ltd. of their film *The Loves of Mary, Queen of Scots.* By this time, however, cinemas were springing up all over Edinburgh and audiences didn't really see the point in going to the theatre just to watch a film. The experiment proved unsuccessful, even though the star of the film, Fay Compton, was one of the most popular actresses of her time.

Three years later, in 1927, Fay Compton appeared at the Lyceum in the flesh, playing her most successful part, the title-role in Barrie's *Mary Rose.* This strange and moving play, regarded by many as the most profound piece of work that Barrie ever did for the stage, has long been a popular favourite at the Lyceum, where it was revived as recently as 1981. In 1927, however, there were two additional reasons for its popularity, one being that Fay Compton, sister of Sir Compton Mackenzie, was the daughter of the actor-manager Edward Compton, whose company had been so popular a generation earlier. Secondly, the part of Cameron, the student-gillie used by the author to rag the English so ruthlessly in the island scene, was played by an Edinburgh actor, Halliday Mason. The tone of *The Scotsman* review was quite different from that which had been assumed in the case of Jack Buchanan and Fred Astaire.

> The situation in which the young mother, spirited away and so deprived of the joy of seeing her child grow up, remains 'earth-bound' in the deserted house, seeking for something the exact nature of which she has forgotten, is, as everyone knows who has seen the play, worked out with a skill which reaches the undoubted level of genius. Miss Compton's acting was equal to the requirements of this exalted achievement in poetic drama.

The plays of J. M. Barrie, of course, have always had a special appeal in Edinburgh. Ever since *The Professor's Love Story* in 1904, all of Barrie's major plays have found an audience at the Lyceum, some of them, like *Mary Rose*, being performed on numerous occasions, even after their author had gone out of style elsewhere. Since Barrie was a graduate of Edinburgh University who had, during his student days, written theatre reviews (had the Lyceum opened just a year earlier, he would undoubtedly have reviewed the first productions) this is not really surprising. Apart from the Theatre Royal in Dumfries, which he visited regularly in his schooldays, Edinburgh was the city in which Barrie received his theatrical education. As a consequence, he wrote many plays which so suited the Lyceum that the theatre might almost have been built for them.

Prior to her creation of the role of Mary Rose, Fay Compton had appeared (although not at the Lyceum) in the title role of Barrie's most popular play of all, *Peter Pan*. So, too, had another actress whose great beauty, fine stage presence and sheer style epitomised the grace and elegance of the West End of Edinburgh in those days. If Barrie was the perfect playwright for the Lyceum, Gladys Cooper must surely have been the perfect actress. Although she had first appeared at the theatre in musical comedy — playing the role of Sadie Van Tromp in a George Edwardes production of *The Dollar Princess* — by 1928 she had moved on to straight drama and, in the March of that year, was seen in a more characteristic role, that of Leslie Crosbie in Somerset Maugham's *The Letter*, under her own management. In this production, *The Scotsman* described her acting as 'an admirable example of dramatic art, marked on its technical side by fine elocution and perfect naturalness of action, and temperamentally realising the subtlety and intensity of the character'.

Charismatic personalities always defy description, of course, but Daphne du Maurier, in an essay she wrote in 1974, came very near to capturing a sense of the effect Gladys Cooper had on her audiences. In the early nineteen-twenties,

Daphne du Maurier's father, the equally charismatic Sir Gerald, appeared with Gladys Cooper in Frederick Lonsdale's comedy *The Last of Mrs Cheyney* at the St James's Theatre. Daphne du Maurier, a child at the time, describes the scene after a performance:

> Now there were two sets of fans waiting at the stage-door after a performance. His and hers. And if nobody screamed or fainted when Gladys finally emerged, I do recollect the murmur that arose from her excited adorers, gradually swelling in volume as she passed between them, and hands would be stretched out to touch her coat as though the very texture had magic properties. Gladys smiled, and waved, and made a dash for her car. . . .

This was exactly the kind of adulation that was apparent in the West End of Edinburgh at this time. It seems highly appropriate, indeed, that Gladys Cooper should have appeared at the Lyceum in 1928, because this was the year that the theatre underwent a profound change, in both policy and management, that would lead to a direct response to the kind of demand that a star like Gladys Cooper created.

By this time, F. W. P. Wyndham was over seventy years of age and his fellow managing director, George T. Minshull, was only a year or two younger. The previous year, 1927, the board of Howard & Wyndham Ltd. had appointed Charles Gulliver as an additional managing director, presumably in preparation for the retirement of the two others. If this was indeed the intention, it did not work out, because Gulliver resigned after only a year in the job. When Wyndham and Minshull finally retired in 1928, A. Stewart Cruikshank emerged as the sole managing director of Howard & Wyndham Ltd.

Wyndham kept his seat on the board and retained an interest in the business for the next two years, until his death in 1930. It is reasonable to assume that he viewed the appointment of the new managing director with a degree of satisfaction, since he had taught Cruikshank everything that he knew about the business of theatre. As for Cruikshank himself, he had his own considerable qualities to add to all that Wyndham had to teach.

Cruikshank was, by any standard, a remarkable man. The son of a master joiner and builder, he had himself served an apprenticeship as a joiner and had come into the theatre, as mentioned in a previous chapter, entirely by accident. Although Howard & Wyndham Ltd. had taken over the management of the King's in 1908, the company did not actually own the theatre until twenty years later, when Cruikshank became managing director. Quite obviously, therefore, Cruikshank's name will always be most closely associated with the theatre that he helped — physically — to build, owned for twenty years and made the centre of all his operations for twenty years thereafter. After his tragic death in a car accident in 1949, a small plate was put up in his memory in the King's, a modest but appropriate tribute to a great manager and impresario.

A. Stewart Cruikshank: Wyndham's protege, Cruikshank was one of the influential impressarios of his day. He began his working life as a joiner and only came into the theatre by chance.

According to Charles Tripp, a former manager of both the King's and the Lyceum, Cruikshank's great talent was for personnel management. He knew nothing at all about the production or artistic side of the theatre, but he had the knack of picking the best people and getting the best out of them, always knowing when to give talent its head and when to draw rein on its enthusiasm. In financial affairs, he applied the rigid logic of the market place. He would not grudge the spending of hundreds of pounds on a costume if he could be convinced that it was necessary, but he was quite capable of sacking any office junior who wasted a penny too much on the postages. In short, he was a man who knew what he was doing, knew what he wanted and knew how to get it. Not for nothing did the employees of Howard & Wyndham Ltd. bestow on him the soubriquet that their counterparts in London had given George Edwardes a generation earlier. To his staff, A. Stewart Cruikshank was always known as 'The Guvnor'.

As an Edinburgh man, born and bred, Cruikshank understood the special ambience of the West End. As a theatre manager, he also understood the basic principle that the key to success in any theatre lies in the relationship between any performance and its potential audience. Four years earlier, a company called the Macdona Players had taken the Lyceum for a period of three weeks in July, in order to perform a short season of plays by George Bernard Shaw. They had been successful enough to return the following year and, when they did, *The Scotsman* welcomed them in the following terms:

> The Macdona Players, in their Bernard Shaw repertory, are assured of a welcome in Edinburgh. A gratifying interest was aroused by their performance a year ago. Since then they have successfully presented Shaw plays in Paris, and have made Shaw seasons popular in London and other English centres. In accordance with the innate tendency to paradox, which seems to be associated with the author, what is regarded as the 'off' season in theatre in Scotland is not unlikely to become the 'on' season in respect of the drawing capacity, during the summer weeks, of the Shaw plays.

The Macdona Players were directed by Esmé Percy, an accomplished and versatile actor who had been one of Benson's proteges and who had also worked in Tree's company. Other members of the company included Howieson Culff, George E. Bancroft, Vivian Beynon, George Larchet and Margot Drake — not exactly household names, either then or now, but good, professional actors whose ensemble playing was polished and most effective with the Lyceum audience.

In the summer of 1928, the Macdona Players' season was followed by another, similar, company, Robert Fenemore's Masque Theatre. Unlike the Macdona Players, the Masque Theatre did not restrict itself to one playwright, but presented 'a season of plays by well-known authors'. Among their first productions at the Lyceum were Barrie's *Dear Brutus*, Strindberg's *The Father*, A. A. Milne's *To Have the Honour* and Chekhov's *The Cherry Orchard*. Although they were probably unaware of it, these two companies were reviving a Lyceum tradition that Howard had initiated back in the eighteen-eighties. As *The Scotsman* had predicted, this form of theatre became very popular.

It is not difficult to discern the reasons for the appeal of these companies for the Lyceum audience of the 'twenties. They were professional without being commercial, entertaining without being vulgar, serious without being too heavy or obscure. In short, they seemed to represent all the values of quality and style with which the West End of Edinburgh was identified in the nineteen-twenties. Only one element was missing and, this being so, the next step was obvious. The argument for a resident company, playing in the theatre for a substantial part of the year, became irresistible.

Whether or not these thoughts occurred to Stewart Cruikshank in quite the manner in which they have been presented is something which, in all likelihood, will never be known. There is no doubt, however, that the new managing director of Howard & Wyndham Ltd. had a very clear idea of the part the Lyceum should play as a theatre within the group. After Cruikshank's accession, any suggestion of the second-rate was dismissed out of hand and the quality of visiting productions rose quite perceptibly. For instance, when that great musical *The Desert Song* first appeared on the Lyceum stage, it did not do so (as *No, No, Nanette* had done) as part of a provincial tour, but was a direct transfer of the original Drury Lane production. Cruikshank knew only too well how important it was to maintain the Lyceum's individuality and sense of style.

Cruikshank knew that a resident company would be right for the Lyceum, but he also knew that it would have to be a very good resident company, run by somebody with the right degree of experience and expertise. With his great talent for selection, Cruikshank had little difficulty in finding the right man for the job. His name was Jevon Brandon-Thomas and the activities of his company were to play a major role in what was to be the most exciting and successful period of the Lyceum's history to date.

5 A Brighter Sunshine

Economic recession, mass unemployment, political crisis leading to the creation of a National Government, constitutional crisis leading to the abdication of Edward VIII, civil war in Spain and the rise to power of Adolf Hitler in Germany all combined to make the nineteen-thirties one of the most dangerous and depressing decades of recent history. It is one of the great ironies of the human situation that the theatre, so often struggling for its very existence in happier, more affluent times, should always flourish in such periods of hardship, uncertainty and apprehension. In so many ways, the Lyceum has never enjoyed a more popular or successful time than it did during the years from 1930 to 1939.

Partly, of course, this was due to brilliant and dynamic management. After Stewart Cruikshank took over in 1928, each of the Howard & Wyndham theatres were subjected to firm policy directives. The spirit of eclecticism which had flourished so long at the Lyceum would be maintained, but henceforth it was to be given a much clearer focus. The advertising described the theatre as 'Scotland's Theatre of Tradition and Edinburgh's Family House' and, in 1932, a policy statement committed the Lyceum to 'the best work of modern writers, together with the classics of the past'. At the same time, opera, pantomime, most of the big musical shows and, eventually, touring productions of Shakespeare were transferred to the King's. Responsibility for carrying this policy out was given to John L. Masterton, one of the most capable and popular of all Lyceum theatre managers.

At this point, something needs to be said about the work of the theatre manager. Although the Lyceum, in common with most other theatres of the time, had no resident company and

Mr Cochran's Young Ladies: C. B. Cochran, the legendary impressario, joined the Howard & Wyndham board in 1930. Here, a typical Cochran chorus is seen in rehearsal.

rarely promoted its own productions, this does not mean that the theatre was simply a building that was available for hire to anyone who could afford the rent. One often reads of such-and-such a management 'taking' such-and-such a theatre, but this was not really as simple as it sounds. The programme for the year required a degree of planning and the theatre manager had to be satisfied that the companies which wished to take the theatre were the right companies for his audience. At the same time, it was very much the theatre manager's responsibility to ensure that visiting companies played to the highest possible capacity audience. Quite obviously, therefore, the audience was the theatre manager's main pre-occupation and the job had to be filled by someone who knew the audience intimately and had a feeling for their response to a particular performance. At that time, most theatre managers had either been actors or had had some connection (often through their families) with the production side of theatre. Cruikshank departed from this tradition by appointing theatre managers who came from the other side of the footlights. Few of these managers had any experience of production, but all of them had a sound business sense (often they were accountants) and would impose financial discipline on the activities of the theatre. Masterton, like other Howard & Wyndham theatre managers, held the firm conviction that the financial stability of the business was the rock upon which success, in production terms, was built. At the same time, he was fully aware of the fact that financial success at the Lyceum depended very much on the quality of the production on the stage.

Robert Donat: The great film star first appeared at the Lyceum in the twenties with Sir Frank Benson's company. He is pictured as Charlie Cameron, with Doris Fordred, in Bridie's 'The Sleeping Clergyman'.

Another important appointment which was made at this time was that of the legendary impresario, C. B. Cochran, who was appointed to the Howard & Wyndham board in 1930. This was the beginning of Howard & Wyndham's London operation — a London office had been opened in 1928, the same year that Cruikshank became managing director — and it was probably due to this connection that many of Cochran's large-scale, spectacular musical shows transferred directly to Edinburgh from London. Most of these, of course, went to the King's rather than the Lyceum, but sometimes (particularly at Christmas, when the King's was in the throes of pantomime) the older theatre would be preferred. One such occasion was the staging, in 1932, of Cochran's London success *The Cat and the Fiddle*, with music by Jerome Kern and book and lyrics by Otto Harbach. This show, however, was not a transfer, but a completely new production in which the leading role was played by Bruce Carfax, an Edinburgh actor and singer who was currently one of Cochran's most popular leading men.

The Cat and the Fiddle, as a musical play, is fairly typical of its kind and not much need be said about it. Set in Belgium, the story revolves around the writing of an opera called *The Passionate Pilgrim*. Apart from Kern's score (which includes the song *She Didn't Say Yes*), the Edinburgh production had the added attraction of a troupe of Belgian actors who had been specially imported to play a number of minor parts. Part of the dialogue being in French, the management were concerned that the accents were authentic. If this fact seems faintly absurd — not many of the audience, after all, could be expected to recognise such authenticity and, of those, few would really care about it — it does demonstrate the lengths to which the management was prepared to go to ensure that the Lyceum's reputation for quality was maintained. Another indication of this, albeit a rather snobbish one, can be seen in the fact that the Marchioness of Queensberry was engaged to design the costumes.

No effort seems to have been spared, it seems, to ensure that the lights of the Lyceum glittered as brightly as possible at this time. Even the touring productions which played the theatre had to be of the utmost quality, as the most random examination of these years will demonstrate. There were Nora Delaney and Dunscombe Branson in *The Barretts of Wimpole Street*; John Gielgud's company in *Musical Chairs* by the brilliant young Scottish playwright Ronald Mackenzie; Barrie Jackson's company (with Robert Donat as Charlie

Cameron) in Bridie's *The Sleeping Clergyman*; Ion Swinley in the first of H. V. Neilson's Shakespeare Festivals. Most of all, there was one of the most popular plays of the time, particularly in Edinburgh — Harker and Pryor's *Marigold.*

Marigold, a simple love story set in Victorian Edinburgh, had been a huge success in London in 1928, when the parts of Mrs Pringle and Marigold had been played by Angela Baddely and Jean Cadell respectively. The touring production that had played the Lyceum in the same year had featured Jean Clyde and Sophie Stewart in these parts and had made a huge impact. Five years later, an actor called Graham Pockett put together a company to revive the play at the Lyceum. It is a measure of the extent to which the Edinburgh audience had taken this play to its heart that, although only five years old, it was described in the following review as an 'old favourite':

> At a time when many a good play and gallant company are faced with half-empty houses and poor box-office returns, the old favourite 'Marigold' can count on a bumper audience and a hearty welcome. The reception given to the Scots comedy last night, on its return to the Lyceum theatre, proved that the firm hold that it has taken of Scottish playgoers, proverbially hard to please, is well maintained. 'I cannot tell you what a thrill we get out of playing "Marigold" to an Edinburgh audience,' said Jean Clyde, in response to repeated calls at the close of last night's performance. Judging by the applause, the thrill was entirely mutual.

That review (from *The Scotsman*) also provides us with a clue to the reasons behind all the vigorous effort that was going into the Lyceum at this time. Once sound was added to film, the cinema really took off and became, for the first time, a serious threat to the city's theatres. This threat could only be countered by investing the theatre with a degree of glamour and spectacle that the cinema could not match. The opening years of the decade were dominated by three glittering and memorable gala nights which had the effect of doing just that.

The first of these took place on the 11th July 1931, when King George V and Queen Mary attended a performance of Barrie's *The Admirable Crichton*, presented by the Masque Theatre, with Esmé Percy in the title role. This was an historic occasion, the first Command Performance in Scotland since 1822, when George VI had attended a performance of *Rob Roy* at the old Theatre Royal. It is small wonder that *The Scotsman*, on this occasion, paid as much attention to the audience as it did to the play.

> The theatre rapidly filled as the time of Their Majesties' arrival approached. The Lord Provost, Sir Thomas Whitson and Lady Whitson and Miss Whitson, took their places in the centre of the front row of the dress circle. The Earl and Countess of Elgin, with Lady Victoria Wemyss and Lieutenant-Colonel the Hon. D. Bruce, were on the box on the right nearest the stage. Harriet, Lady Findlay, D.B.E., chairman of the Board of Managers of the Royal Infirmary of Edinburgh, for the building fund of which Their Majesties instructed the command performance, occupied the centre box with a party of friends. The Sheriff of the Lothians, Sheriff Brown, with his guests, was in the third box on the right. Interest centred on the vacant box opposite. The division between the two

furthest from the stage had been removed
so as to form a single box: and the three
had been lightly draped in pale green and
gold, harmonising with the upholstery and
decoration of the rest of the theatre.
Meanwhile the large orchestra played their
preliminary selections from 'The Geisha',
'Songs of the Hebrides' and Elgar's 'Pomp
and Circumstance'. The audience conversed,
or examined the souvenir programme, with
its front page in purple, red and gold, and
containing an appeal by the Lord Provost
for the Bi-Centenary Extension Fund of the
Royal Infirmary, a history of the Royal
Lyceum Theatre, an appreciation of the
Masque Theatre and the Repertory
Movement in Scotland, along with the
playbill of the evening. It was an occasion
well worthy of a souvenir programme. The
auditorium, seen from the front of the
stage, made an exhilarating spectacle. Never
had such an audience assembled in the
theatre. The gallery, the only unreserved
portion, was filled, as were the other parts
of the house, with an eager throng, the first
of whom had arrived to form a queue at
half-past eight that morning.

The Royal occasion, however, was
historic in another sense, being the first of many
that the Royal Family were to make to the Lyceum.
The next would be three years later, but before that
there was to be another night which, although very
different in character, was no less glittering in its
sense of occasion. This was the celebration of the
Lyceum's semi-centenary, which occurred on the
10th September 1933. The play chosen for the
jubilee week was *Sally Who* with Jessie Matthews.
Although the show, a musical revue, demonstrated
that the theatre had come a long, long way from
Henry Irving, this was an occasion in which the
prevailing mood was nostalgic and celebratory of
the Lyceum's traditions. This mood is best caught
in an article by a regular playgoer of the time,
Daniel James McArthur, which appeared in the
Edinburgh Evening Dispatch during jubilee week.

Of that wonderful partnership of Henry
Irving and Ellen Terry I write with
hesitation, as I saw him only during the last
ten years of his life; but the beauty of
Becket, the subtleness of *Hamlet*, and the

92

intensity of *Macbeth* and *The Bells* remain with me today, a glorious memory. And who does not recall Martin Harvey's tremendous success in *The Only Way* and *The Breed of the Treshams*? I recall with pleasure also Ben Greet . . . Joseph Haviland, Herman Vezin and Louis Calvert in sound Shakespearean seasons. Marie Tempest in *The Marriage of Kitty* and Irene Vanburgh in *Trelawney of the Wells* and *The Gay Lord Quex* are still a happy memory to many middle-aged playgoers. Mrs Patrick Campbell was a frequent and welcome visitor, and her *Voodoo, Hedda Gabler* and *Magda* were magnificent performances; recalling not only her famous earlier success as *The Second Mrs Tanqueray*, but her meteoric rise to fame from the ranks of the Colchester amateurs in the early 'nineties. To Arthur Bourchier and Violet Vanburgh we owe many splendid plays. In *At the Villa Rose, Treasure Island, The Land of Promise* and *Find the Woman*, each found parts worthy of their gifts.

The first tour of Matheson Lang and Hutin Britton in *Mr Wu* was an overwhelming success, although, personally, I liked him best in *Carnival*. There was a virile Petruchio by Oscar Ashe . . . while William Gillette as *Sherlock Holmes* and E. S. Willard in Barrie's early play *The Professor's Love Story* are worthy of remembrance. And all those delightful Barrie women whom we took straight to our hearts on their first appearance — Hilda Trevelyan, Pauline Chase, and Fay Compton, to name but three of the best-beloved — are they not still, happily, in our thoughts.

There is a certain significance in the fact that all the names that McArthur mentions, both famous and forgotten, were active in the field of straight drama and there is no doubt that there was an immediate association of the Lyceum with the straight play. This being the case, it seems rather inappropriate that the semi-centenary should have been celebrated with a musical revue, even though it did feature the most popular actress of her time.

The following year, 1934, the King and Queen visited the Lyceum on the occasion of a charity performance in aid of the Royal Infirmary and the Princess Margaret Rose Hospital for Crippled Children. Once more there was a distinguished audience, including one theatrical figure who had come near to attaining the rank of royalty himself. In fact, at one point during the long wait of the excited crowds around the theatre, this great performer was actually mistaken for the King.

> Long before the Royal party were due to arrive the approaches to the theatre were thronged. The animated scene as the audience were assembling passed the time agreeably for the waiting crowds. A long line of motor cars stretched into Spittal Street and beyond, and around the entrance to the theatre there was a stir of orderly bustle as the elegantly-gowned ladies and gentlemen in evening dress alighted. Ladies and gentlemen, possibly too impatient to complete the motor car crawl to the entrance, arrived on foot. Crimson carpets were laid across the pavement to the three doors, and the facade of the theatre was tastefully decorated with baskets of ivy-leaved geraniums and marguerites. The sound of cheering from the east end of Grindlay Street shortly after eight o'clock set up the cry of 'Here they come!' from those in the crowd nearer the theatre, but the cheers were for Sir Harry Lauder, who could be seen in his car garbed in Highland costume. The famous comedian waved his handkerchief cheerily to the crowds.

The play that the King and Queen were to see that evening was *The Enchanted Cottage* by Sir Arthur Pinero, a writer who had had an early association with the Edinburgh stage and, indirectly, with the Lyceum. As a young actor, Pinero had been a member of R. H. Wyndham's stock company at the Adelphi. Rather more interestingly, however, the play was presented by a company whose work would dominate the history of the Lyceum for the next twenty years. Founded and led by Jevan Brandon-Thomas, the son of the author of *Charley's Aunt*, they were originally a touring company, performing under the title of 'The Brandon Thomas Seasons'. The Brandon-Thomas Company usually described itself as a 'repertory' company and, before going any further, it is important at this point to discuss that term.

The original, continental, meaning of the word referred to a company of actors who would rehearse a repertoire of plays which would then be presented for a season, playing a different play on different nights of the week. In the British context, this system has never worked properly, except in the most unusual circumstances — at the National Theatre, for instance, which is a repertory theatre in the true sense of the word — and the term has generally been misused in this country, referring to a theatrical philosophy rather than a method of presentation. When the first British repertories were established — in Birmingham, Liverpool and Glasgow — the aim had been two-fold: to move away from the romantic theatre of the nineteenth century towards the new naturalism of Ibsen and Shaw; and to establish a theatrical presence which would be completely independent of London. As the Repertory Movement grew, two additional characteristics began to develop. First, the most viable form of production was found to lie in a new form of touring. The companies would play in a theatre for a season of several weeks rather than a single week. Secondly, naturalistic writing led inevitably to a naturalistic style of acting, pioneered most notably by Sir Gerald du Maurier in the

The Lyceum in the Thirties: The view from the Dress Circle, prior to the alterations of 1935. In those days, the theatre had a seating capacity of 2,500.

'twenties, which proved to be extremely popular. This style of acting does not really allow for one or two major performances to be fed by several mediocre ones, but rather requires ensemble playing of a very high order. Repertory actors, therefore, attained a collective popularity rather than individual ones.

As described in the previous chapter, the first repertory companies to visit the Lyceum were the Macdona Players and the Masque Theatre. These two companies and one other (the St Martin's Players) played seasons at the Lyceum in 1931 and 1932. The Jevan Brandon-Thomas company played their first season at the Lyceum in 1930, taking the theatre for six weeks, during which they performed two Noel Coward plays (*The Queen was in the Parlour* and *The Young Idea*), two by Brandon-Thomas himself (*Passing Brompton Road* and *The Glory of the Sun*), John Van Druten's *Diversion* and Augustin MacHugh's *Officer 666*. The company then returned south, playing a number of successful seasons in Bournemouth.

Three years later, in 1933, they were asked to return. It is quite clear that Cruikshank, having looked at what was available in the repertory field, had made his choice. In 1933, the Jevan Brandon-Thomas season was not of fixed duration, but had been put on a month's trial. In a short history of the company which he wrote in 1936, Brandon-Thomas describes how the relationship with Howard & Wyndham Ltd. began:

> And so we returned to the Royal Lyceum Theatre, Edinburgh, for a month's trial season. And one of the things that cheered us most was the fact that we were still remembered after three years by many who had witnessed our first visit. For the first month our fate hung in the balance and there were moments of despair. To add to our worries, though to others' enjoyment, Scotland experienced its first heat-wave for thirty years. Still we clung on and gradually business went up and up. . . .
> The season ran that year for fourteen weeks. We could stay no longer for the autumn was already booked with touring companies, so Howard and Wyndham

Jevan Brandon-Thomas: The master of repertory. Actor, director, playwright and publicist, Brandon-Thomas created a huge audience for his company in the thirties.

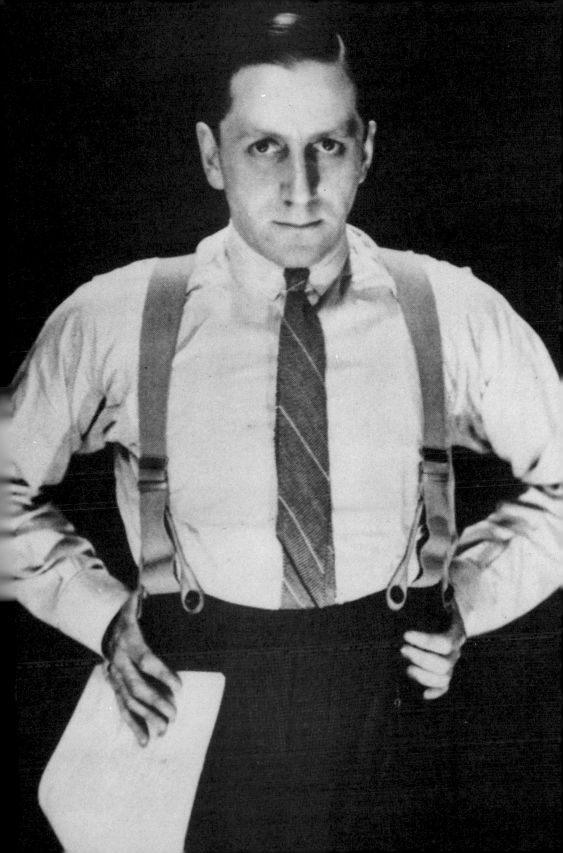

suggested that we should try our luck at the Theatre Royal, Glasgow. There we opened in September. It proved the hardest struggle of any theatre we ever tackled, but after the first anxious weeks the business started to move. Howard and Wyndham were patience itself, our season was extended, and business grew at every performance. That Christmas we paid our last visit down south before settling in Scotland.

Thus began a pattern of operation which was to be sustained over the next two decades, with the resident repertory company playing part of the year in Edinburgh, part of the year in Glasgow.

It was a good system, but it did not run itself. It required to be operated by someone of sense and ability, someone who knew the theatre business inside out and who was prepared to work very hard at it all the time. Jevan Brandon-Thomas was just such a man. Under his guidance, the Brandon-Thomas Season was extended from

Phoebe Kershaw: This beautiful actress took part in a little bit of television history, when she played in 'First Stop North' by Nicholas Phipps, the first repertory play to be televised.

Enid Sass: One of the most charming of Brandon-Thomas's leading ladies. She later became a founder-member of the Wilson Barrett company.

fourteen weeks in 1933 to thirty-seven weeks by 1937. During that time, the company had similar success in Glasgow.

The secret of the company's success was based on two things: the development of a strong acting team and the creation of a close relationship between the company and the audience. Although there were no stars — Brandon-Thomas was fond of saying that every member of his company was a leading actor — some were obviously more popular than others. Among a whole galaxy of attractive, accomplished and personable actresses — which included Enid Sass, Kitty de Legh, Phoebe Kershaw, Margot Lister and Phyllis Barker — the most popular of them all was unquestionably Joan Kingdon, a founder-member of the company and an actress of great beauty, talent and personality. One of Joan Kingdon's most endearing idiosyncrasies, it seems, was a certain tendency to commit spoonerisms and during one performance of Noel Coward's *The*

Phyllis Barker: A fine dramatic actress who stayed with the company for most of her stage career. Her greatest success was in 1949, when her "Hedda Gabler" created a sensation at the Gateway.

Young Idea there was one instance of this which was talked about for years afterwards. Playing the part of a young wife who is about to leave her husband, she had the following exit-line:

> Just a moment, I'm just going to get my hat and coat.

Instead of which, she said:

> Just a moment, I'm just going to get my cat and hoat.

Smiling to the audience, she ducked her head in apology — and said:

> I'm sorry — I mean my hoat and cat.

She got it right the third time, but it was this kind of failing, with its touch of eccentricity, that the Edinburgh audience loved. Like so many other actresses of her generation, Joan Kingdon retired from the stage when she decided to marry, giving what was to have been her last performance at the Lyceum on the 26th October 1935. A few weeks prior to this date, patrons at the theatre received the following letter, slipped inside their programmes.

> *Miss Joan Kingdon's Presentation*
> Avonside, Eskbank, Midlothian.
> 16th October 1935
>
> Dear Sir or Madam,
> Many of Miss Joan Kingdon's admirers, who had enjoyed her lovely performances with the Brandon-Thomas Seasons at the Royal Lyceum Theatre, Edinburgh, have approached us with a view to receiving subscriptions to permit of a suitable gift being made to her on the evening of her farewell performance, on *Saturday, 26th October*, prior to her marriage.
> It has been suggested that by this means they would be enabled to show her, in tangible form, their appreciation of the very many pleasant evenings spent at the Theatre.
> Contributions of any amount should be sent as soon as possible.
> Yours faithfully,
> C. Belford Melville (Convener).

In the event, no gift was actually purchased. In a simple ceremony on the Lyceum stage after Joan Kingdon's final performance — playing the part of Helen Pettigrew in Balderston

Joan Kingdon: the most popular Lyceum actress of the thirties, seen here with Wilson Barrett and Jevan Brandon-Thomas. Joan Kingdon's spoonerisms endeared her to the Edinburgh audience.

and Squire's eighteenth-century fantasy *Berkeley Square* — Jevan Brandon-Thomas presented the actress with a cheque for £33:6s, the proceeds of the subscription. The extent of Joan Kingdon's popularity can be gauged from the fact that the cash collected was made up of sums ranging from pounds to pennies, the subscribers coming from every walk of life, from the lady volunteers at the Blind Asylum to the workers at the North British Rubber Company.

This kind of thing typifies the *kind* of popularity that the company enjoyed. An actress like Joan Kingdon might be talented and beautiful, but she was not remote and fabulous — she was a friend towards whom the audience was prepared to make the kind of gesture that they would normally reserve for friends. To achieve such a relationship in Edinburgh — where the people, though friendly, can seem off-hand and cold to strangers — was no mean achievement.

As for the men in the company, they were held in no less regard. The earthy Irish actor, George Larchet, the distinguished Stephen T. Ewart, the sturdy Owen Reynolds and the handsome Kenneth Hyde all had their particular admirers, but there was one name that would always stand out above the others on any Brandon-Thomas cast list — that of Wilson Barrett.

There is a story about an old lady

who, on coming to the theatre to buy tickets, was introduced to Wilson Barrett. 'Oh!' she said. 'Are you any relation to the *famous* Wilson Barrett?' Realising that she meant the Victorian actor-manager, the actor informed her that he was, indeed, the great man's grandson. 'In that case,' said the old lady, 'perhaps you can tell me something? Who *was* the famous Wilson Barrett?'

As the years went by, Wilson Barrett was to demonstrate that he had inherited a great deal more than simply acting talent from his famous grandfather. At this time, however, he was, quite simply, the best actor in the company. Brandon-Thomas declared that the only weakness Barrett had was a tendency to 'put both feet in it' if he was bored by a part — a failing that Brandon-Thomas sought to avoid by carefully choosing the parts that Barrett played. Even so, like the other actors in the company, he would play an extremely wide variety of roles during any one season.

Any Brandon-Thomas Season was a time of exceedingly hard work for all concerned. During the course of 1935, for instance, the company produced no fewer than thirty-one plays by a wide variety of authors, including Barrie, Coward, Maugham, Priestley, Arnold Bennett, John Drinkwater, Frederick Lonsdale, Arnold Ridley and Harold Brighouse. In addition to those, there were several new plays, often by Scottish authors like Donald Carswell, Robins Millar, William Templeton and Elizabeth Drew. Since each play would receive no more than a week's rehearsal, followed by a week's performance, an actor would generally have three parts on his hands at any point in the season — the part he was playing, the part he was rehearsing and the part he was about to rehearse.

Jevan Brandon-Thomas's personal contribution to the season was enormous. Actor, director, playwright and business manager, he also found time to handle the company's public relations, writing a great number of articles about the company for any publication which was prepared to print them. Besides contributing to the local press and to Howard & Wyndham's own magazine, *The Courier*, there was often a Brandon-Thomas article in the week's theatre programme. The following is a short extract from such an article, entitled *Early Experience*, which appeared in 1936.

> Although we work very hard, there is a lighter side to stage life and some of my experiences, when I look back on them, seem very amusing, though at the time I was more frightened than amused.
>
> My first concerns a theatre cat which wandered on to the stage one night in a serious play and curled itself up in a comfortable armchair in full view of the audience. It was perfectly quiet throughout the scene and all would have been well had it not been for the fact that the heroine, after an impassioned speech, had to sit on the self-same chair. I whispered a warning under my breath which she did not hear, I made signals to her, I even made faces at her, but the scene proceeded to its usual climax and she fell, sobbing on to the chair and on to the cat which with one wild screech leapt through the fireplace to the accompaniment of roars of laughter from the audience.
>
> It was in 'The Rat' that I played a bold bad Baron and was discovered with the heroine in my arms with Ivor Novello who played the hero. As I saw him over the girl's shoulder I had to back to the table, seize a large carving knife that was lying on it, and rush at him with murder in my heart. On the first night, instead of responding to my acting he stood helpless and weak with laughter. I stood in astonishment and looked round to find that by mistake I had picked from the table, not a carving knife but a large tablespoon!

The above is fairly typical of the kind of piece that appeared regularly in the programme of the 'thirties, not only from Brandon-Thomas but from other members of the company and even, occasionally, from members of the audience. These programmes were really well-edited little magazines, full of articles, stories, jokes, recipes, household hints and poems. More than any other surviving material, they communicate to posterity the atmosphere of intimacy and sense of belonging that was evident in the theatre at that time. Fringe

103

This much was proved most conclusively in the early summer of 1936, when the company had what proved to be, not only their own greatest success, but the most successful production that the Lyceum has seen this century. The play, moreover, was not a classic, but a completely new play, written by a member of the company, Margot Lister. Based on the life of Mary, Queen of Scots, *Swords About the Cross* was an ambitious, hugely expensive production, employing a cast of thirty-three actors, plus an equivalent number of supers, with incidental music played by the internationally renowned Elizabethan ensemble, the Dolmetsch Orchestra.

The play tells the story of Mary's life from her girlhood in France to her execution in England, covering the tempestuous events of her Scottish reign in seven intervening scenes, making nine scenes in all. Perhaps the most controversial element in the play is the author's treatment of Darnley's murder by the explosion at Kirk o' Field. This was based on a book that had been written some years earlier by General Reginald Mahon, entitled *The Tragedy at Kirk o' Field*, in which it had been argued that both Mary and Bothwell had been innocent of any plot to murder Darnley. According to the theory expressed by General Mahon, Darnley's death had been an accident, that he had placed the gunpowder in the house himself, with the express intention of murdering Mary. This was a topic of discussion which received much attention in those days.

The part of Mary was played by a pretty young actress called Nancy Hornsby, Darnley by Wilson Barrett and Bothwell by Jevan Brandon-Thomas himself, standing in for Owen Reynolds, who had taken ill at the last moment. Well down the cast, in the tiny part of Kirkcaldy of Grange, was a young Scottish actor, James Donald, who would later, despite illness, make a substantial career in films. Unlike most Brandon-theatre groups today often use the phrase 'people's theatre', but repertory companies like the Brandon-Thomas Seasons fulfilled this phrase more completely than anything that has been seen since.

Thomas productions, *Swords About the Cross* ran for two weeks rather than one, but that tells only half the story. The demand for tickets was so great that four extra matinees had to be added in the first week — on Tuesday, Wednesday, Thursday and Friday — making eighteen performances in all. Taking every performance into account, the play was seen by 42,000 people, a figure which assumes even greater significance when one realises that the previous year (1935) the management had instituted alterations to the building which had reduced the capacity from 2,500 to 1,650. Somehow or other, an extra 650 people were accommodated in the theatre every night and the play achieved the amazing percentage of 125 per cent of capacity for the run of the play.

Press coverage of the play was extensive and *Swords About the Cross* made a small piece of broadcasting history. On the opening night, 25th May 1936, Robin Stark gave an eye-witness impression of the event for the Scottish Home Service — the first time that this had ever been done in Scotland.

Both artistically and financially, *Swords About the Cross* was a great success. The following year, the company sought to repeat their success with a pageant play in honour of the

105

Coronation of George VI. This was called *Drake* and had been written by various hands to commemorate the great Elizabethan hero. Some successes, however, are just not repeatable, the Edinburgh public could not get as excited about an English pirate as they had about a Scottish Queen, and *Drake* signally failed to make any appreciable impact. The company did have one outstanding success, however, later in the year, when they produced their first Shakespeare. Wilson Barrett scored a substantial success as the Prince in *Hamlet*, with Joan Kingdon making a popular (although temporary) return as Ophelia.

Presenting Shakespeare was a very risky business in those days — ten years later Cruikshank was to ban the Bard at the Lyceum — and it says much for the company's following that they were able to make a success of it. That year, the Brandon-Thomas Seasons ran for a record thirty-seven weeks and everything seemed set fair for the future. Then, most unfortunately, Cruikshank and Brandon-Thomas quarrelled.

All that is known for certain about this sad disagreement is that three people were involved — Cruikshank, Brandon-Thomas and a young Scottish actor called Alex Macalpine, who later went to London, changed his name to Simon Lack and carved out a highly respected career in stage, broadcasting and film. Since all these three are now dead, the nature of the quarrel will probably never be known and must forever remain a matter of speculation. In any case, the most important aspect of the quarrel was its result: the contract between the Brandon-Thomas company and Howard & Wyndham Ltd. was terminated and the gains of the previous four years quite simply evaporated overnight.

Brandon-Thomas had made a success of his Lyceum seasons by dint of artistic flair, sound managerial judgement and sheer hard work. If Cruikshank thought that another company could simply replace the Brandon-Thomas Seasons without a serious loss of business, he was mistaken. The company, moreover, would take some replacing. By this time, repertory dominated the

Lyceum's programmes. Taken together with the Christmas show, it accounted for all but six playing weeks in the year. It was extremely doubtful if another touring repertory company, starting from scratch, could be found to fill the space that Brandon-Thomas had left.

Cruikshank tried to solve this problem by setting up his own company. Under the leadership of actor/director Ronald Adam, the Howard & Wyndham Players took the stage of the Lyceum in the spring of 1938, the first time a similarly named company had done so since the death of J. B. Howard forty-four years earlier. Although they were a professional, highly talented company — including such names as Frank Harvey Jr., Sonia Dresdel, and a young John le Mesurier — the Howard & Wyndham Players were not a success and were together for only two seasons. No doubt they were faced by many problems — not the least of which was the lack of time in which to build an audience — and no doubt Ronald Adam worked every bit as hard as Jevan Brandon-

Thomas, but when one looks at the short history of the company, one cannot help but wonder at some of the curious judgements that were made regarding choice of plays.

Two examples, one from each season, will serve to demonstrate this failing. At the end of the first season, the company presented a new play by Frank Harvey Jr. entitled *Saloon Bar*. This was a large-scale ambitious piece of social realism, set in a London public house, with a cast that included Norman Claridge, John Franklyn and Mona Glynne. Ronald Adam, whose publicity statement predicted that this play would be 'the most important event of Edinburgh's theatrical year', made the following observation on the play's setting:

> Bars in London are different from those in
> Scotland. Their atmosphere is more social,
> and they are not so completely concerned
> with the business of drinking as they are
> here. The very presentation of this
> atmosphere, which is a little strange to us,
> is therefore interesting in itself.

Now, to begin with, a theatre audience is never satisfied with something that is simply 'interesting'. The best of plays, particularly in the field of social realism, will either involve the audience or it will alienate them. One suspects that the latter was the case as far as *Saloon Bar* was concerned. The play cannot be faulted for this, but its chances were not aided by the statement. It is always a grievous error to tell any Scottish audience — in the theatre or anywhere else — that the English have something better than they have!

The second example comes from 1939, when the company produced Barrie's last play, *The Boy David*. On the face of it, this would appear to have been a good idea, since the play had had its opening night, amid scenes of almost hysterical excitement, at the King's only four years previously. Unfortunately, the fact that the original production had been seen so recently tended to work against the Howard & Wyndham production. In place of Elisabeth Bergner — for whom the play had been written — the title role was played by Victoria Hopper, who had to compete with the un-favourable comparisons that were inevitably made.

Once more, as in the case of *Saloon Bar*, the play was faced with disadvantages before it even opened.

These strictures, of course, are made with hindsight and are probably more than a little unfair. They have not been made without purpose, however, since they help to put the achievement of the Brandon-Thomas Seasons into perspective. In the 'thirties, it became clear that repertory was the key to success at the Lyceum. Apart from the glittering and glamorous occasion of the kind described earlier in this chapter, it was the only form of theatre which could really respond to the challenge of the cinema. Indeed, the practice of changing the play every week meant that the theatre was able to exploit the new social habits of the cinema-going public, who were seeking public entertainment to a greater extent than ever before. Repertory, however, was an extremely specialised business, demanding something more than simply theatrical talent. Besides skill, dedication and an ability to endure an almost impossible workload, it required a deep understanding of the paying audience. Jevan Brandon-Thomas had possessed all these qualities and, as the decade drew to a close, it seemed that he would never be replaced.

At this time, of course, the people of Edinburgh, no less than their counterparts everywhere else, had other things on their minds. As the war-clouds gathered over Europe, there was great uncertainty regarding the future of mankind, never mind the Lyceum Theatre. On the 3rd September 1939, war was declared and, once again, the world was to undergo a complete and irrevocable change. By a curious coincidence, the Brandon-Thomas company were in Edinburgh on the day that war was declared, not at the Lyceum of course, but at the Empire. In less than two years, however, they were to return to their old stamping-ground, with a new leader and under a new name. Over the next fifteen years, they were to develop into the finest acting team in the British Isles and to become a Scottish institution. To a great many people, even today, mention of the Royal Lyceum Theatre will prompt immediate memories of the Wilson Barrett Company.

Waves of Goodwill

> I have never, in all my experience, known
> anything quite like the warmth of a Scottish
> audience to players whom it likes. It has
> nothing to do with the applause — that one
> gets everywhere in varying degrees — but
> nowhere else that I know of do you get
> those waves of goodwill which you can feel
> coming across the footlights to you. I have
> played long runs in London, I have played
> long resident seasons in towns all over
> England, but nowhere else have I
> experienced that emotional contact which
> we all know so well in Edinburgh and
> Glasgow.

The story of the Royal Lyceum Theatre in the nineteen-forties (and much of the 'fifties) is bound up almost wholly with the story of the Wilson Barrett Company. Apart from one other event — which is important enough to deserve a chapter to itself — the company's Spring and Autumn Seasons constituted the highlights of most of those years, occupying the theatre for an annual total of eight months at this time.

In the beginning, the company had simply been the Brandon-Thomas Seasons, minus Jevan Brandon-Thomas. After his departure from Scotland, Brandon-Thomas had returned to London, where he had taken the King's Theatre, Hammersmith and the Wimbledon Theatre, meaning to do there what he done so successfully in Edinburgh and Glasgow. It was a daunting prospect, but he had found a backer to lend him the necessary working capital and he was confident of eventual success. Unfortunately, at the last moment, this backer had let him down and, in spite of spending every penny of his own, he had been forced to close down. In the early spring of 1938, the Brandon-Thomas Seasons wound up and eight years of quite splendid achievement came to an unhappy end.

Wilson Barrett as Hamlet: Like his grandfather before him, Wilson Barrett was an actor-manager in the true sense. His company eventually became a Scottish national institution.

Then, quite unexpectedly, another backer approached Wilson Barrett (who had been a director on the Brandon-Thomas board) and offered to supply the necessary finance if he, Barrett, would take over the company. At first, Barrett hesitated — he had had, after all, no experience of business at this time — but, encouraged by the support of Esmond Knight, he finally decided to give the idea a year's trial and, on the 24th January 1939, 'Wilson Barrett and Esmond Knight Ltd.' opened its first season at the King's Theatre, Hammersmith, with Noel Coward's triple bill *Tonight at 8.30*. Apart from Barrett and Knight, the cast of that first production included many names which would have been instantly recognisable to Lyceum audiences of that time — Enid Sass, Kitty de Legh, Phyllis Barker, Owen Reynolds, George Larchet and Neil Crawford.

That first season was a considerable critical success and lost less money than had been expected. (The creation of a new repertory company involves the creation of a new following, and a loss of £2,000 had been expected. In the event, the company lost less than £200, which was really a considerable gain.) Most of the plays presented were popular favourites of the time — one or two of them, like Emlyn Williams' *Night Must Fall* and Noel Coward's *Private Lives*, retain a measure of popularity even today — but there were two plays at least which gave some indication of the adventurous spirit that would characterise the company's activities in the future. The first of these was an American play, David Belasco's *The Return of Peter Grimm*, directed by Jevan Brandon-Thomas. This had become quite famous in the U.S.A., but it had never been seen in England before, so presenting it was something of a gamble. An even greater gamble was the first production of a completely new play, Nicholas Phipps' *First Stop North*, which made a considerable impact and, had it not been for the outbreak of war, might even have gone on to score a major success. As it was, *First Stop North* earned the distinction of being the first play by a repertory company to be televised, the B.B.C. transferring the entire production from

Hammersmith to Alexandra Palace and giving the whole play a live transmission one afternoon in May 1939.

After the first successful London season, the return to Scotland was immediate. George Black, manager of the Empire, booked the company for a nine-week season and they were given a rapturous welcome back by the Edinburgh audience. There was not an empty seat in the house and, as each of the cast made his or her first entrance, the play was held up for minutes at a time by the sustained applause. That season was no less interesting nor successful than the London one had been. Among the plays presented were Pinero's *The Enchanted Cottage*, Dodie Smith's *Autumn Crocus*, Barrie's *Quality Street*, Rattigan's *French Without Tears* and a new play by an old Edinburgh favourite, *Mind Over Murder* by Joan Kingdon.

As was mentioned in the previous chapter, the company were at the Empire when war was declared, and it was for this reason, more than any other, that their residence in Scotland became permanent. The original intention seems to have been to base the company at the King's, Hammersmith, in the spring and autumn, and to go out on tour during the summer. On the outbreak of war, however, every theatre in the country closed and there was a state of chaos in which it was impossible to make any definite plans. Over the next year or so, the company found themselves in serious difficulties, scrambling all over the place for any kind of booking. To make matters worse, on the 5th November 1940, while travelling between Bristol and Edinburgh, Wilson Barrett was involved in a serious accident, when the train in which he was travelling collided with another. His spine was crushed and his pelvis fractured in two places and he was to be out of action for many months.

As he was later, with hindsight, to admit, this enforced rest did Wilson Barrett a power of good. For two years, his every waking moment had been filled with the effort and worry of keeping the company in business. He had been under enormous strain, both physically and mentally, so his accident proved, in this respect at least, to have been a blessing in disguise. As for the company, they were all back in London and, by a series of accidents, they were able to stay together until the following May, when they were due to open at the Glasgow Alhambra for a twelve-week season.

It was this season which really settled the future of the Wilson Barrett Company. They did so well there that Stewart Cruikshank asked them to take the Lyceum for a six-week trial season in September. Their welcome back was no less enthusiastic nor triumphant than it had been at the Empire two years previously, with the result that the season was immediately extended until Christmas. From then on, a pattern was set and the fortunes of the company stabilised. Throughout the next decade or so, they would play the Lyceum from February to May, move to the Glasgow Alhambra (and, after 1948, Her Majesty's Theatre, Aberdeen) where they would stay for the summer, returning to the Lyceum from September until Christmas.

This all sounds fairly straightforward, but, of course, it was not — particularly in the early days, when there was a war going on. The Second World War, no less than the First World War, made a major impact on the nature of British society, even though its effects were, perhaps less cataclysmic than those of the earlier conflict. It was a time of great shortage and the Wilson Barrett Company, like every other commercial enterprise, suffered badly from a lack of men and materials. The search for young leading actors was bad enough — all the young men being in uniform; Barrett tells us that he was reduced to interviewing 'hunchbacks, cripples, schoolboys and old gentlemen between sixty and eighty', but materials for set-building were completely unobtainable. In spite of this, however, Barrett was determined that standards should not suffer, arguing that it was during this time of adversity that they should be at their highest. Accordingly, in the spring of 1943, the company produced their first Shakespeare, *Romeo and Juliet*. One of the problems with this production, which was directed by Clare Harris, was the balcony scene. The company did not employ a designer at this time and, lacking the right materials, they were at a loss to determine how the play could be staged. In his history of the first ten years of the company, *On Stage for Notes*, Wilson Barrett tells how this problem was solved.

> About a month before our production was due, John Gielgud was in Edinburgh playing in 'Love for Love', and he and Clare being old friends, she gave a supper party for him in her rooms one night after the show, during which we happened to mention our difficulties. We didn't leave Clare's that night until after one o'clock, but by eleven the next morning Gielgud was in the Lyceum. During our morning break for coffee he gave Clare a design for a standing setting (which he said was a combination of an early production of his at Oxford, when he used the bare Elizabethan stage, and of his recent elaborately built production at the New Theatre in London) and a sheaf of notes indicating where each scene could be played. I can't think that he had had time to sleep at all that night, but the result was brilliant.

Although *Romeo and Juliet* received extremely good notices (Alan Dent of *Punch* described it as 'the best production of the play we have ever set eyes on') it was not a financial success, Shakespeare being bad box-office at the time. Other plays in the season, however, had done very well and the financial health of the company was fairly sound — so much so, in fact, that when financial crisis threatened its very existence shortly afterwards, the Wilson Barrett company survived.

The backer whose original investment had enabled Barrett to get the company going again became worried by the course the war was taking and decided to withdraw his support. A very large sum of money had to be found to repay him and Barrett only just managed to do so by selling everything that he owned and risking a charge of fraudulent management by opening his Glasgow season with an overdraft of £600 at the bank. After that, however, the financial state of the company never looked back, going from strength to strength during the remaining twelve years of its existence.

The fact that he managed to operate at a profit — with no sponsorship or Arts Council subsidy of any kind — often led to Wilson Barrett being criticised for being 'too commercial'. This peculiar charge, which carries with it the suggestion that anything that is enjoyed by a great many people must, *for that reason*, lack quality, has its origins in the artistic snobbery that began to be applied to theatre in the 'forties and which, unfortunately, is still with us today. In Barrett's case, it is a charge that is plainly absurd. He was never in the business of theatre simply to make money — most of the profit, in any case, went straight back into the company — and, had he chosen to do so, he could have much more easily made a financial success out of his own acting career. Far from being a profit-seeking entrepreneur, Wilson Barrett was an idealist who had only taken on the role of manager in order that his own concept of theatre should be given life. Like his grandfather before him, he was an actor-manager in the truest sense of that expression.

At the same time, as far as Edinburgh was concerned, he had to be very careful. At the Lyceum, he found an audience which, although warm and enthusiastic, could scarcely be described as adventurous in their theatrical tastes. Keen on quality, but suspicious of experimentation, they were not an audience upon which new ideas could be easily tried out. An analysis of the company's Edinburgh productions reveals that, between the years 1941 to 1951, out of a total of two hundred and seventy-one productions, only six new plays were produced at the Lyceum. Nor did the classics fare much better, since only thirteen productions (mostly Shakespeare) came into this category. Some thirty-seven plays had Scottish or Edinburgh connections — the most notable being George Scott-Moncrieff's *The Fiddler Calls the Tune* and Alexander Reid's first play *Worlds Without End*, both new plays at the time — and something like twice that number was made up of contemporary successes which are now largely forgotten. The great bulk of the productions, however, consisted of twentieth-century plays by authors whose names are instantly recognisable — Shaw, Barrie, Maugham, Priestley, Bridie, Rattigan and (most popular of all) Coward. In that these authors have always been considered safe bets at the box-office, Wilson Barrett's Edinburgh productions could be described as 'commercial'.

These facts, however, somewhat miss the point as far as the aims and ideals of the Wilson Barrett Company were concerned. Although they were always concerned to perform work of quality, it was the quality of the performance rather than the quality of the writing which was their foremost concern. The motivation that lay behind their endeavours was put most succinctly by their original founder, Jevan Brandon-Thomas, in an article that he wrote for *The Courier* in 1935.

> In London, the practice of long runs, where plays achieve some three or four hundred performances, is excellent for the box-office, but not usually good for the quality of acting. I remember my father telling me how difficult it had been to maintain his performance in *Sweet Lavender*, which ran for two years in the original production in London. It is humanly impossible (or, shall we say, almost impracticable) that an actor or actress can maintain the high standard of his or her performance without becoming in some degree mechanical. It is impossible to achieve genuine emotion in a highly strung scene night after night for three or four hundred consecutive performances. Nowadays, atmosphere plays such an important part that it essential to have no jarring note in the presentation of a play. It is like a jigsaw puzzle in which every piece must fit exactly, however small that piece may be. Nothing is more difficult to achieve than a perfectly balanced cast, but it is a goal worth striving for, and my humble belief is that here Repertory can give great help to the theatre. For it is by virtue of the fact that artists in a Repertory Company play together so long and are in such close contact with each other that they achieve a team spirit which is invaluable to the life of the theatre.

There is no doubt that the regular members of the Wilson Barrett Company were unstinting in their dedication to the theatrical philosophy expressed above. Without such dedication, there is no doubt that the company would simply have failed to function, as Wilson Barrett himself acknowledged in an emotional passage in *On Stage for Notes*. Describing the members of his company as 'real actors', he explained.

> When I say 'real actor', I don't mean good actor or bad actor, success or failure, but simply the men and women who love the theatre so much that they will suffer any hardship so long as they can be a part of it. This driving power gives them the strength to cope with poverty and squalor: they leave comfortable homes and live in digs (and what some of these digs have been like, the last few years especially, only actors know): their nearest and dearest die, but they don't miss a performance: they go to the theatre so ill that they can hardly get their make-up on their faces, but nobody in front would ever guess: they work sixteen hours a day in Repertory Theatres throughout Great Britain, and enjoy it: they devote their whole lives to the theatre, often, at the end, with lamentable financial results. These are the real actors, and these are the people of whom my own company has always been largely composed and, I hope, always will be.

Among those 'real actors' was an actress of whom Barrett was especially fond. Indeed, when he was writing the above, he might well have been thinking of Kitty de Legh, to whom he always referred as 'our dear Kitty'. In 1940, she had been playing the lead in Gerald Savory's *George and Margaret* when her husband, Caleb Porter, had suddenly died. Apart from the fact that she did not miss a single performance, Kitty de Legh came straight from her husband's funeral service to a special rehearsal which had been called for another actress who had agreed to stand in — at very short notice, there being no understudies in those days — for one of the other parts. A former member of the original Brandon-Thomas company, Kitty de Legh stayed with Barrett more or less continuously through the 'forties until, finally, ill-health forced her to retire. She settled in Edinburgh for many years, living in her Thistle Street flat.

Another Wilson Barrett stalwart was J. Caswell Garth, the company's business manager. Not really an actor, Garth nevertheless often found himself on the stage, particularly during the war years, when no one else was available. As business manager he had, of course, a great deal of work to do, so he never had any time to learn lines, having to get by with cribs which were pasted all over the set. One of the most famous of these was a Latin grace which he had to deliver while playing a priest. This he had written upside-down on his shirt-front, so that he could deliver it with his head bowed! On another occasion, some of the younger actors in the company played a rather cruel trick on Garth by mixing all his cribs up, as a result of which the play came to a dead stop and the young actors in question found themselves in serious trouble.

One of these young actors was Robert James, something of a matinee idol in Edinburgh at that time. Since his days with Wilson Barrett, James has gone on to a distinguished acting career in films and television. He is by no means the only former member to have done so. Sometime around 1941 (Barrett was never quite sure when or how) a 'small, and in spite of everything her parents could do, exceedingly dirty schoolgirl' managed to join the company on the stage of the Glasgow Alhambra. Two years later, she joined the company as a permanent member and was with Barrett for most of the rest of his time. Today she is a very successful television producer and her name is Pat Sandys.

In 1947, another Glasgow youngster joined the company, playing the part of the Player Queen in *Hamlet*. His name was Lawrence Dalzell and Barrett discovered him while he had been producing his own company of young players in scenes from Shakespeare. Dalzell had written to Barrett, inviting him to come and see the show, but since Barrett was busy at the time, he had sent Clare Harris in his place. Her first impression of the young actor is worth repeating.

> Well, dear, he certainly has all the attributes of a big star. All his scenes were played in a spotlight in the centre of the stage with everybody else down-stage in the corners with their backs to the audience.

Like so many other young actors who were later to make a name for themselves in the theatre — and the list includes Doreen Andrew, Joan Benham, Richard Mathews, Geoffrey Palmer and Nicholas Parsons — Dalzell spent his formative years with the company. Today, he is one of our most influential theatrical agents.

Robert James, Pat Sandys and Lawrence Dalzell have something else in common, however, besides their former membership of the Wilson Barrett Company — they are all Scots. Partly due to wartime shortage, partly to his own inclinations — he was always sensitive to and understanding of Scottish aspirations — Wilson Barrett recruited many of his actors locally and gave much encouragement to emerging Scottish acting talent. Scottish drama and the Lyceum's place in its history are subjects which will be discussed in a later chapter, but at this point it is worth noting that a great many talented Scottish actors made their first appearance on the Lyceum stage as members of the Wilson Barrett Company. Apart from those already mentioned, Madeliene Christie, Jameson Clark, Brown Derby, Helena Gloag, Edith McArthur, Bryden Murdoch and John Young all appeared with the company during this time. One young Scottish actress, Elizabeth Sellars, became something of a film star, while another, Jacqueline Mackenzie, made a similar impact in the field of television. Perhaps the most talented of all, however, was a young man who Barrett very nearly turned down. On the recommendation of Pat Sandys, who had seen him in an amateur production, Barrett agreed to give this young actor an interview. Finding him extremely gauche and possessed of a Scots accent that was so thick that he could hardly understand a word of it, Barrett might easily have sent the young actor packing, had he not had a vacancy in stage management at the time. He took him on in the capacity and thus began the theatrical career of Walter Carr, one of the finest of all Scottish actors.

The company's productions were usually directed — or 'produced' as they used to say in those days — by either Barrett himself, Richard Mathews, Clare Harris, Joan Kemp-Welch or, later, C. B. Pulman. Although a company style evolved over the years, they were all very different in their approach. Clare Harris (whose tragically early death from cancer left all who knew her shattered) tended to be quiet, thoughtful, methodical with all her ideas worked out before rehearsals began. Joan Kemp-Welch, on the other hand, tended to improvise a great deal, keeping all her creativity for the actual rehearsal, often allowing a flash of inspiration to alter her original concept. Perhaps the most interesting of the directors, however, was C. B. Pulman, a Yorkshireman and something of a polymath, being an author, playwright, painter, poet, dialect specialist and art and drama critic. Although he directed a great many plays for the company, perhaps his most notable achievement was the Festival of Britain production of his own adaptation of Beaumont and Fletcher's *The Knight of the Burning Pestle* in 1951.

Over the fourteen years in which they played the theatre, the relationship between the Wilson Barrett Company and the Lyceum audience became closer and closer. Eventually, it reached the point where Barrett's intimate knowledge of the Lyceum audience meant that the company could practically do no wrong. Just how well Barrett knew his Edinburgh public is revealed by a rather interesting programme note that he wrote for a

1951 production of Elsa Shelley's *Pick-up Girl*. This American play, a court-room drama involving prostitution, would probably seem quite innocuous by the standards of today, but was regarded as very controversial material to present in Edinburgh at that time. In his programme note, Barrett made a direct appeal to two qualities that he knew the Lyceum audience had in abundance — a high sense of moral justice and a devotion to the Crown.

> The locale of this play may be set in America, but unhappily the appalling facts are just as applicable throughout Great Britain today, and the chance that this production may help, even in the smallest way, to open complacent eyes to the horrors that are going on in our midst is our justification for presenting this play, which we know will shock and disgust many people. If, however, Her Majesty, Queen Mary could go out of her way to see *Pick-up Girl*, then we feel that no one has the right to say that this play, however painful they may find it, should not be played.

Pick-up Girl was the hit of 1951.

As far as Howard & Wyndham Ltd. were concerned, the success of the Wilson Barrett Company fitted in admirably with their plans for the Lyceum. They built up a steady public at the theatre, providing a firm base on which the management could build at other times of the year. This was particularly important during the war, when a visit to the theatre could be a very risky business. The programmes of the early 'forties carry a warning which seems a little alarming

> Air Raid Warning
> You will be notified by the Manager if a warning is given. Do not be alarmed because the warning does not mean that a raid will take place and it is not likely to occur for at least five minutes. If you wish to leave for home or the nearest shelter, you are at liberty to do so, if not remain in the building, which is much safer than the streets.

Edinburgh, however, mercifully escaped all but the most occasional bombing and the Lyceum stayed in business continuously throughout the war years, during which time

'Scotland's Theatre of Tradition and Edinburgh's Family House' maintained its reputation for quality theatre.

The tone was set early on, with three productions of quite outstanding merit appearing in the theatre in the last months of 1939: Edith Evans and Ronald Squire in a new production of Shaw's *The Millionairess*; John Gielgud and Beatrice Lillie in an anthology evening entitled *Plays and Music*, featuring scenes from the work of authors as diverse as Shakespeare, Coward, Gordon Daviot and Herbert Farjeon; and Herbert Marshall's production of Ardrey's *Thunder Rock*, with a strong cast led by Alec Guinness and including Bernard Miles and John Mills. As has already been mentioned, Shakespeare was not considered good box-office either before or after the war, but when Donald Wolfit's company arrived with *The Merry Wives of Windsor* in 1940, they had a sensational reception. This production, which was described by *Punch* as 'a romp with the flowers of handsome speech and movement', carried echoes of Tree and the Terry sisters in that it featured Wolfit himself as Falstaff, with Irene and Violet Vanburgh as Mistresses Page and Quickly.

There was another (although rather different) Shakespeare performance the following year, when Sybil Thorndike and Lewis Casson appeared in an Old Vic production of what is possibly the least-known of all Shakespeare's dramas, *King John*. In 1942, a quite different tradition was represented when A. E. Matthews appeared with Marie Tempest (something of a grande dame by this time, but just as glamorous and just as stormy as she had been in the days when she cut up George Edwardes's trousers) in a production of St John Ervine's *The First Mrs Fraser*. The great Viennese tenor, Richard Tauber, played the part of Schubert in a 1943 production of *Blossom Time* (originally entitled *Lilac Time*, this is a version of the composer's life which makes use of his own music), while Zena Dare, Roger Livesey and Ursula Jeans arrived the following year with what was then a very new play, Lillian Hellman's *Watch on the Rhine*. Finally, in 1945, the end of the war was celebrated by the appearance of five ex-P.O.W.s in a Colditz-style revue entitled, appropriately enough, *Back Home*.

All of these were, of course, touring productions which were seen in a great many other places besides the Lyceum and, as such, their connection with the history of the theatre is relatively slight. In a number of cases, however, this connection is closer than it may, at first sight, appear. The independent producers who had dominated the theatre world during the 'twenties gradually gave way in the 'thirties to limited companies whose financial structure was based on the issue of share capital. The gamblers, in other words, had given way to the businessmen. At the same time, under the leadership of Cruikshank, the firm of Howard & Wyndham Ltd. had continued to grow. By 1945, they controlled bookings at no fewer than eighteen British theatres (seven of which they owned outright), had a controlling interest in Moss Empires Ltd. and a considerable financial stake in the following production companies: H. M. Tennent Ltd., Charles B. Cochran Ltd., Linnit and Dunfee Ltd., Henry Sherek Productions Ltd., Bertie A. Meyer, David Mayer & Co. Ltd.

The financial strength of these companies enabled them to put the most profitable shows on the road and, by virtue of their stake in them, Howard & Wyndham Ltd. naturally brought such shows to their Edinburgh theatres. Many of these were large-scale musicals which the Lyceum might not have otherwise been able to afford, such as *Annie Get Your Gun* (starring Peggy Powell), *Brigadoon* (with Bruce Trent), *Carousel* (with Edmund Hockridge), and, most intriguing of all, the first stage version of *Snow White and the Seven Dwarfs*, featuring 'the World's Smallest Actors'.

Apart from these productions, however, there was a great deal of straight drama of a very high quality. For example, the spring season of 1950 began with the Old Vic Company in one of the best-remembered of all their productions of *Hamlet*, in which Michael Redgrave played the Prince. This was followed by the great Swedish actress Signo Hasso in Ibsen's *Rosmersholm*, followed in turn by the equally famous American solo performer, Ruth Draper, with her one-woman show. Finally, Evelyn Laye and Frank Lawton (with a young Edinburgh actor called Tom Fleming in the cast) appeared in a play called *September Tide* by Daphne du Maurier.

It says a great deal for the Wilson Barrett Company (who were, of course, playing in the theatre throughout this period) that they could be seen in such a context and not be considered in the slightest degree second-rate. The average playgoer does not always discriminate between this company and that — it is all the Lyceum to him — and, given the number of famous names that have been mentioned in the last few pages, it would have been quite understandable if a weekly repertory company had had difficulty in holding their own in such company. Yet the Wilson Barrett Company not only held their own, they prospered during these years. Indeed, there is a sense in which their presence in the Lyceum was crucial to the theatre's well-being in the nineteen-forties and 'fifties. It was they who preserved the Lyceum's identity, they who responded so successfully to the week-by-week challenge of the cinema (which was then, of course, at the very height of its popularity) and it was they who kept audience attendance at a viable level. Far from being made to look inferior by visiting celebrities, those celebrities often found that *their* performance was being judged by standards that Wilson Barrett had over the years taught the Lyceum audience to expect.

Yet, ironically, the most important single development which took place during their time at the Lyceum was one from which the Wilson Barrett Company were to be forever excluded. Since this was a development which was to lift the Lyceum's status to a new international level, it must now be considered in a fresh chapter. Before doing so, however, it is appropriate at this point to mention the regrettable fact that, despite their excellent record in Edinburgh, Glasgow and everywhere else they played, the Wilson Barrett Company never received an official invitation to appear at the Edinburgh International Festival.

Wilson Barrett as Lob: The Plays of J. M. Barrie have always found a good audience in Edinburgh, the city where their author received his theatrical education.

7 An International Stage

There is a legend that the Edinburgh International Festival of Music and Drama began at a tram-stop in Princes Street in 1939. Rudolf Bing, so the story goes, was on his way back to his hotel after taking part in a touring production of *The Beggar's Opera* with the Glyndebourne Opera at the King's Theatre. Waiting for his tram, he looked up to see the ramparts of the Castle bathed in moonlight and was immediately reminded of Salzburg. 'The idea of a Festival,' according to Robert Ponsonby, one of Bing's successors as Festival Director, 'was born at that moment.'

This is a nice story — which very possibly contains more than a grain of truth — but it over-simplifies the origins of this great cultural event to the point of misrepresentation. The Edinburgh Festival was not born as the result of a sentimental whim, nor had Bing's motives for creating it, in the first instance at least, anything to do with the City of Edinburgh, moonshine on the Castle ramparts notwithstanding. In the Souvenir Programme for 1971, he made a fairly straightforward statement of what these motives were.

> England has been starved of international art and artists for five years; thus I thought of an international festival of orchestral music, great soloists, drama, ballet — and opera — Glyndebourne Opera! Where could such a festival be held? Near London, I thought, it would have to be . . . Cambridge or Oxford . . . but I could not get anybody interested.

Edinburgh, however, *was* interested — indeed, not only interested but enthusiastic. (This is a point which continues to escape those people — among them a certain section of the press which has always found good copy in using the Festival as a whipping-boy — who argue that the Edinburgh Festival has nothing to do with Edin-

The Great Duncan Macrae: Seen here in a Festival production of 'Let Wives Tak Tent', Robert Kemp's free translation of Moliere's 'L'Ecole des Femmes'. Macrae's natural projection made him the centre of any stage he stepped upon.

burgh but has been imposed on the city by outsiders.) Towards the end of 1944, Bing discussed the matter with H. Harvey Wood, the British Council's Edinburgh representative, who immediately put the matter up to the Lord Provost, Sir John Falconer. Less than a year later, preliminary arrangements for the first Festival were complete. At the time, it all seemed (and, indeed, *was*) terribly risky: there was no telling whether it would be a glorious success or a disastrous failure. Not surprisingly, a number of commentators were sceptical. Sir Thomas Beecham made a speech in Glasgow which prophesied 'a perfect fiasco', while one Scottish newspaper warned that the Festival would breed 'long-tailed squanderbugs'. Without the benefit of our hindsight, such critics could not perceive that the Edinburgh Festival was exactly what Europe needed after five weary years of war — a shot in the arm which would raise morale in that grey time of post-war austerity.

In Edinburgh, the ground for the Festival had been prepared during the preceding years, while the war was still in progress. During this time, the city had played host to a large influx of visiting soldiers and refugees from all over Europe. These visitors found a native population that was warm in its welcome and considerate in its attendance to their needs. Organisations such as the W.V.S. Allied Information Bureau in Princes Street did much valuable work in this respect, providing translations, organising dances and other social events, putting relatives in touch with each other and promoting classes in everything from typing to map-reading. As far as the cultural requirements of the visitors were concerned, the British Council became heavily involved, with Harvey Wood arranging lunchtime recitals, readings and (with the help of the Scottish poet Edwin Muir) discussions by leading British writers. These were the true roots of the Edinburgh Festival.

At the end of the war, while the Festival was still in the planning stage, an event took place which must have done much both to silence the critics and to steel the resolve of the Festival's founders. On the 16th July 1945, for the first time in two hundred and sixty-five years, the Comédie Francaise visited Scotland, playing for a week at the Royal Lyceum Theatre. They presented four plays — *Le Tartuffe, L'Impromptu de Versailles, Phédre*, and *Le Barbier de Seville* — and were received enthusiastically by the Lyceum audience, playing to excellent houses throughout the week. At the civic reception which was held in their honour, the Lord Provost made a speech in French, of which the following passage is a translated extract.

> Your fame has long preceded you. We know your illustrious history, dating from the days of Louis Quatorze and extending some 260 years. The world famous names which adorn your roll are household words in this country. We know the great things you have achieved for art and literature, and how through the centuries you have worked to preserve the highest standards. In doing so, you have enriched not merely your own nation, but the world of culture.
>
> Our countries, once so linked together in history, are now again united by the bonds of adversity. We feel towards each other that sympathy and comradeship which is produced by common trial. Let us increase those feelings and use them to cement our friendship so closely that never again shall we do other than work together in harmony for the common good of the world.
>
> I hope we will cultivate frequent visits such as this, and extend them into a permanent friendship and constant exchange of visits. Thus, by understanding each other better, we will appreciate each other more. By a common devotion to the arts, which ennoble and elevate, we can leave behind the realms of misunderstanding and help to create a world of happiness and peace.

The above passage (and particularly the last paragraph) can be seen as a neat expression of the philosophy which has informed and sustained the Edinburgh International Festival of Music and Drama since its inception. Not even Sir John Falconer's later, perhaps better-known description of the Festival as 'a common meeting-place for all the peoples of the world and a source of spiritual refreshment for all who are weary of war'

129

can better it is a summing-up of the Festival's philosophy and ideals.

Although this is not the place to give a full account of the Festival's history — or even, at this point, a complete appraisal of the Lyceum's part in it — the fact that the Comédie Francaise played the theatre two years before the Festival began ought to demonstrate how clearly the Lyceum was committed to the event. Cruikshank was an original member of the Festival Council and the Lyceum has featured as one of the key sites for Festival drama since the beginning. Indeed, in 1946 (still, of course, a year in advance of the first Festival) the theatre played a part in the kind of interesting theatrical event for which the Edinburgh Festival has become famous.

Jean Cocteau's *L'Aigle a Deux Têtes* is a play of quite haunting beauty which had its premiere in Paris in the autumn of 1946. Prior to this, however, the Arts Council of Great Britain sponsored an English version by Ronald Duncan, entitled *The Eagle has Two Heads*, which made a short tour of Scotland and Wales in the August of that year. At the Lyceum, which was one of the dates on that tour, the audience witnessed a performance of great atmosphere and power. This is how the performances was described by *The Scotsman* at the time:

> An audience, accustomed to the commonplace, may feel that a Queen celebrating an anniversary by dining with her husband's ghost, is a slightly perplexing introduction to a play, but thereafter the story follows the known lines of any melodrama and drives to the usual tragic conclusion. But with the outer story the likeness between this play and melodrama ends. It is a poetic play, and this means that its language is a medium which transfigures it, and which, by the power of imagery and paradox and, in this instance also, by symbolism, ennobles it, destroying the time factor. Thus, last night, this story of a Queen who makes of the poet and revolutionary who enters her bedroom to assassinate her, her lover and her destiny, and whose tragedy is set in the middle of last century, might have been that of Mary

Stuart, or any other heroine of high romance. . . . The atmosphere in which this Queen of Shadow and Death moves is that of Maeterlinckian drama rather than of Shakespeare's more human world. But there is no doubt that, in the Queen, Cocteau has written a memorable part.

When the play opened in Paris, the part of the Queen was created by Edwige Feuillere and the poet by Jean Marais. In Duncan's English version, these parts were played by Eileen Herlie and the same James Donald who, ten years previously, had played Kirkcaldy of Grange with the Brandon-Thomas company in Margot Lister's *Swords About the Cross*.

The French connection was continued when the Festival finally began in 1947, the first overseas company to appear in a Festival production at the Lyceum being that of Louis Jouvet. Jouvet, a disciple of the great pioneer of Modern French Theatre, Jacques Copeau, had been a member of the influential Cartel des Quatre, a directors' co-operative which was formed in 1927 with the stated aim of achieving the 'retheatricalisation' of the French Theatre. Originally something of a visual stylist, Jouvet nevertheless developed an approach in which the text of the play was all-important — 'the text needs to be *breathed*' he used to tell his actors — and is probably best known for his association with two dramatists, Jean Giraudoux and (because he directed his first play, the one-act *Les Bonnes*) Jean Genet.

At the first Festival, Jouvet presented two plays, both of which, interestingly enough, have a Scottish connection. The first of these was Moliere's *L'Ecole des Femmes*, which Scottish playgoers have come to know best in Robert Kemp's free translation in Scots, *Let Wives Tak Tent*. Besides this, there was a modern play, Giraudoux's wistful yet humanistic fantasy *Ondine*, based on a legend which, although current throughout Europe, is particularly common in Scotland. It is the story of the mermaid who enters human society by marriage, learns the ways of men, then returns, in the end, to her own people. A great success when it was first produced in 1939, it was

131

Jouvet's original production which was seen in Edinburgh in 1947.

Another innovative French director was Jean-Louis Barrault, who appeared at the Lyceum during the 1948 Festival with a company led by himself and his wife, the actress Madeliene Renaud. Like Jouvet with Giraudoux, Barrault formed a working relationship with a dramatist, the great poet of the French theatre, Paul Claudel, with whom he explored the concept of 'Total Theatre', most notably in Claudel's *Le Livre de Christophe Colomb*. In 1948, however, this relationship was fairly recent and there was no Claudel in Barrault's season, the first of three appearances he was to make at the Edinburgh Festival. Instead, there was a production of *Hamlet*, Marivaux's *Les Fausses Confidences* and a mime, *Baptiste*, from the Marcel Carne film, *Les Enfants du Paradis*.

Barrault returned to the Lyceum during the 1957 Festival with a production of Anouilh's *La Répétition, ou L'Amour Puni*, but this most theatrical of all French dramatists was first introduced to Festival audiences in 1951, when Le Theatre de L'Atelier (a company which had long specialised in Anouilh's drama) appeared at the Lyceum in two earlier plays, *Le Rendez-vous de Senlis* and *Le Bal des Voleurs*. In the first of these, the central character, Georges, escapes from the dilemma of his life by actually recasting himself in a completely new role during the course of the play. Tired of life with his rich wife, his parents, his friend and his mistress, he takes up with a young girl and, with the use of hired actors, he creates a fictitious world into which they both escape. The second play, *Le Bal des Voleurs*, is no less theatrical. A leading Anouilh scholar, Professor A. D. Howarth of Bristol University, describes it as a 'comédie ballet', expanding this description as follows:

> This is Theatre, interpreted as pure entertainment: an escapist world of fantasy and make-believe, in which the respectable financiers act like crooks (and dress up as *apaches*) while professional pickpockets are seen as honest working men (who dress up as 'grand d'Espagne'). The charade is set going and kept in motion by Lady Hurf,

the first of a series of amiable, eccentric aristocrats who provide the author with a stage persona in which he can exploit all the tricks and surprises at his command. Throughout, there runs the metaphor of life seen as the acting out of arbitrary-assigned roles, for which one must constantly dress up and assume disguises.

As with Giraudoux's *Ondine*, these two Anouilh plays had had their first productions in the 'thirties and, experimental as they had been (and, to some extent, had remained), the passing of the years and the polished performance of a company who had already presented them successfully and who knew them intimately assured their continued success at the Festival. It is noticeable that, in the early years at least, the foreign companies who appeared at the Lyceum avoided doing anything that was completely new, preferring to use both the theatre and the Festival as a showcase for their acknowledged achievements. Besides the French, the first decade of the Festival saw productions from Germany and Italy on the Lyceum stage. In 1949, the Dusseldorf Theatre presented an adaptation of Gounoud's *Faust*, whilst the colourful and exciting Teatro Piccolo Milan appeared in Goldoni's *Arlecchino: The Servant of Two Masters* and Pirandello's *Questa Sera Si Recita a Sogetto* (Tonight We Improvise) during the tenth Festival in 1956. Understandably enough, any new work, experimental or not, was left to the British companies.

Although there were a number of new productions of classics — notably John Gielgud's startlingly original production of *Medea*, with Eileen Herlie in the title role — it was the new plays which created most interest and caused most comment. Indeed, the very first new play that was presented at the Lyceum during the Edinburgh Festival caused so much comment that some aspects of it will probably create avid discussion until the end of time. On Monday, 22nd August 1949, *The Cocktail Party* by T. S. Eliot received its first performance on the Lyceum stage. A Henry Sherek production, it was directed by E. Martin Browne and had an extremely strong cast in Alec

Guinness, Robert Flemyng, Cathleen Nesbit, Irene
Worth, Ernest Clark, Donald Houston and Ursula
Jeans.

The Cocktail Party, probably the most
successful fusion of commercial theatre and poetic
drama that has ever been accomplished, is now
recognised as one of the classic plays of the
twentieth century. At the time of its first production, it received a mixed reception from critics and
audiences alike, something which might well have
been expected, since Eliot has always been the kind
of writer who arouses strong partisan feelings. W.
A. Darlington of the *Telegraph* hailed *The Cocktail
Party* as 'one of the finest dramatic achievements of
our time', while Alan Dent of *Punch* described the
play as 'a finely acted piece of flapdoodle' and Ivor
Brown of the *Observer* called it a 'long, vague
sermon', but prophesied that it would be a
about' by Festival audiences.

Even the most hostile critics tended to
agree with Ivor Brown: the general consensus was
that *The Cocktail Party* was a very important play
and Brown's prophesy has proved correct on both
counts. Nowadays, whenever *The Cocktail Party* is
talked about, discussion tends to centre on the
question of the extent to which Eliot was able to
function as a poet within the context of a conven-
tionally naturalistic play, but in 1949 the burning
issue was one of an altogether more specific nature.
During the party which takes place in Act III, one
of the characters, Alexander MacColgie Gibbs,
relates the death of another, Celia Coplestone. In
the definitive Faber edition, the lines are:

> *Alex* . . . But Celia Coplestone, she was
>   taken.
> When our people got there, they questioned
>   the villagers—
> Those who survived. And then they found
>   her body,
> Or at least, they found the traces of it.
> *Edward* But before that . . .
> *Alex* It was difficult to tell.
> But from what we know of local practices
> It would seem that she must have been
>   crucified
> Very near an ant-hill.

In the original production, however, the audience at the Lyceum witnessed a very different version of this part of the play.

> *Alex* . . . But Celia Coplestone she was
>   taken.
> When our people got there, they questioned
>   the villagers—
> Those who survived. And then they found her
>   body,
> Or at least, they found the traces of it.
> *Edward* But before that . . .
> *Alex* It is difficult to say,
> At such a stage of decomposition:
> Bodies disintegrate quickly in that climate.
> But from what we know of local practices
> It would seem that she must have been
>   crucified
> Very near an ant-hill. They smear the victims
> With a juice that is attractive to the ants.

It was the lines 'juice that is attractive to the ants' and 'at such a stage of decomposition' that caused the furore. In 1949, audiences found such images shocking and extremely distasteful, not to say offensive. After the Festival production, both E. Martin Browne and Henry Sherek pressed Eliot to excise them, which he did for London.

The Scottish poet and critic George Bruce tells an interesting story about *The Cocktail Party* in his history of the Edinburgh Festival, *Festival in the North: the story of the Edinburgh Festival* (Robert Hale, 1975), which gives some indication of the initial effect the play had.

> I recollect attending a cocktail party immediately after the first performance of the play at which opinions were very diverse. The Scottish dramatist James Bridie thought that novelty had been too much sought after, others that the horrible death of Celia was too much for the tone of the play. Into this situation came the author of *The Cocktail Party*, smiling gently as if he had nothing to do with the disturbed opinions. I remarked that I found his *Cocktail Party* was a good deal clearer in meaning than this one. He said — 'I hope so.'

Eliot, one suspects, was simply being polite. Certainly, when it was suggested to him shortly afterwards, by the *Glasgow Herald*, that audiences had not found the meaning of the play to be very plain, he gave the gentle but direct reply — 'Perhaps I did not intend that they should'. Later in that same interview, however, he gave the fullest explanation of his motives that has ever appeared.

> All that one can aim at in a play of this type, which endeavours to combine the dramatic and the poetic in a somewhat new way, is to provide a plot and characters which are on the immediate theatrical level intelligible. . . .
>
> The first and perhaps the only law of the drama is to get the attention of the audience and to keep it. If their interest is kept up to the end, that is the great thing. But there is a more poetic side to it, treating it according to the way in which we treat poetry as distinct from drama. If there is poetry in the play, and I hope there is, then one cannot explain it in the ordinary sense. No explanation in the ordinary sense of a poem is adequate. If you can completely explain a poem, with an exact correspondence between the deliberate intention of the author and the reception of the idea by the reader, then it just is not poetry.

Clearly, Eliot's intention was to create a new poetic drama by bringing the forms and practices of the modern poetic sensibility into the serious theatre. It is something of an irony that the success of *The Cocktail Party* turned out to be a major stumbling block to Eliot's ambition in this respect. In an earlier play, *Murder in the Cathedral* (Mercury Theatre, London, 1935), he had combined 'the dramatic and the poetic in a somewhat new way', using dramatic conventions and devices which were as demanding on his audience as his poetry. Had he sought to develop his drama along the lines indicated by that play, he might well have created a corpus of work on which a renaissance of the poetic drama could have been based — and which would have been, incidentally, entirely appropriate to the new spirit of adventure which was beginning to emerge in the theatre even then. Instead, he turned to a plain, almost naturalistic convention, and the success of *The Cocktail Party* seemed to convince him that this was the right road to take. The result was not exactly disastrous: his subsequent plays, *The Confidential Clerk* and *The Elder Statesman* (both of which had their premiere performances at the Lyceum) are both well-made and interesting dramas, but there is little poetry in either. Eliot, it seems, was seduced, not so much by the theatre, but rather what he imagined the theatre to be. *The Cocktail Party*, far from marking the start of a new and exciting direction in Eliot's work, led him into a theatrical dead-end, even though it will always be recognised as the high-water mark of his drama and one of the great plays of the twentieth-century stage.

Other new plays which had their first production at the Lyceum during the early years of the Festival have not stood the test of time nearly so well. These include Peter Ustinov's *The Man in the Raincoat*, Charles Morgan's *The River Line*, Christopher Hassall's *The Player King* and the first stage performance of Dylan Thomas's magnificent radio play, *Under Milk Wood*. Of much greater interest, however, is the season of three plays (two of which were new) which was presented by the Glasgow Citizens' Theatre in 1950, the year after *The Cocktail Party*. These were *The Queen's Comedy* by James Bridie, *The Atom Doctor* by Eric Linklater and *Douglas* by the eighteenth-century Scottish dramatist, John Home.

Home's play is a rather poor vehicle for the modern stage, owing its fame very largely to a theatrical anecdote concerning its first perform-ance at the Canongate Theatre in 1756. On that occasion, it seems, the play had such an effect on the audience that one galleryite was moved to cry out, 'Whaur's yer Wullie Shakespeare nou?'. The great success that *Douglas* enjoyed, both in Edinburgh and in London, led to Home, a Presbyterian minister, being forced to quit his charge at Athelstaneford in East Lothian and, indeed, to leave the ministry altogether. This was the last occasion on which the Church made a major attempt to suppress theatrical activity in Scotland and, together with the anecdote, accounts for the somewhat legendary reputation that *Douglas* has been accorded in the annals of Scottish cultural

history. Certainly, when one reads the play today, one cannot help but wonder what all the fuss was about. Written in a turgid blank verse, full of bathos, with a plot of quite devastating improbability and a dramatic structure which is just about as basic as it is possible to be (being merely a succession of duologues), the play's one saving grace lies in its central character, Lady Randolph, which is a superb part for an actress of maturity. In 1950, this part was played by Dame Sybil Thorndike, whose son, John Casson, directed the play. Cedric Thorpe Davie composed the incidental music and the play was preceded by a Prologue by Robert Burns. Originally written for the benefit performance of the Edinburgh actor William Woods in 1787, this Prologue was beautifully delivered by James Gibson (who also played the part of Old Norval) and was regarded by many observers as the best part of the play.

As far as the new plays were concerned, both were given a good reception by the

Festival audience, but each divided the Scottish and London critics more or less evenly. Eric Linklater's *The Atom Doctor* (later renamed *The Mortimer Touch*) is a satirical farce, with a plot which aims at a modern version of Ben Jonson's *The Alchemist*. Linklater's flashing wit, aided by two masterly comic performances from Duncan Macrae and Lennox Milne, filled the Lyceum with laughter, but did not impress the critics. The London press acknowledged Linklater's wit and the excellence of the cast, but felt that the Edinburgh Festival was not really the place for such a play. The Scottish press attacked the play ferociously with phrases like 'not up to Festival standard'. Very possibly, they were irritated by the fact that a Scottish writer had been represented at this great international event by such a frivolous play, part of which is concerned with poking fun at a topic as parochial as Scottish Nationalism. They could not see, as George Bruce certainly did, that 'nothing is more liberating from locality than the play of wit and fantasy of Linklater'. It seems that Eric Linklater had embarrassed this section of Scottish opinion. He was always very good at doing that.

The third play, however, is more interesting (and certainly more important) than either of the other two. James Bridie's *The Queen's Comedy* is a spectacular fantasy in which the gods consider the feckless nature of mankind in its pursuit of the futile obscenity of war. The war is the Trojan War, but the soldiers are dressed in khaki and speak in contemporary language, so the play carries many echoes of a much more recent conflict. Directed by John Casson and Tyrone Guthrie, designed by Molly MacEwen, *The Queen's Comedy* produced some fine performances from the Citizens' Company, notably Walter Fitzgerald (Jupiter), Sonia Dresdel (Juno), Duncan Macrae (Vulcan), James Gibson (Neptune), Stanley Baxter (Mercury), Lennox Milne (Minerva), Roddy MacMillan (a Hospital Orderly) and Dorothy Primrose (a Nurse). As far as the press were concerned, the Scottish and London critics were divided as completely as they had been over *The Atom Doctor*, but this time it was the other way around — the Scottish press thought highly of

The Seagull: Dame Judith Anderson and Tony Britton in an Edinburgh Festival production of Chekhov's play at the Lyceum in the fifties.

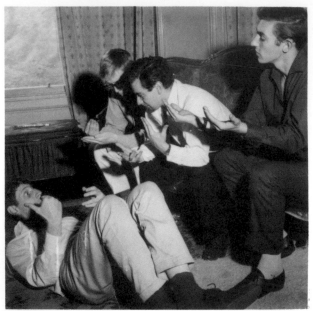

Bridie's play, while the London papers disliked it. 'Somehow it fails to take wing,' wrote *The Times*, '. . . too much argument, a too shadowy logic . . . the comedy is a festival piece, and with the end of the festival should surely have served its purpose.'

Audiences seem to have responded well to the play, despite a rather perplexing ending, since described by Maurice Lindsay as 'ineffectual, if not embarrassing'. The best defence against this charge can be found in a letter that the play's director, Tyrone Guthrie, wrote to Bridie's biographer, Winifred Bannister, quoted in Bannister's *James Bridie and His Theatre*:

> In my opinion, this play is Bridie's greatest work. I think it was not better received because we — no blame to anyone in particular (author, producer, actor *and audience* all responsible) failed to make clear that the play's meaning was explicit in the long, final speech. Audiences long for explanations, for endings which are final, cosy and romantic. This speech says there is no explanation, that there is no finality, and implies that the human-divine situation isn't a bit cosy or romantic. What people *don't want* to understand, they don't hear!

Whether the Festival audience understood *The Queen's Comedy* or not, they certainly came to see it in droves. It is a matter of recorded fact the Glasgow Citizens' Season of 1950 did the most successful business of any of the early Festival seasons at the Lyceum, playing to a figure of 94.5 per cent house capacity. Bearing this in mind, it seems a curious aberration on the part of the Edinburgh Festival that the Citizens' were not invited to return to the Lyceum for many years.

As time passed and the faith of the Festival's instigators — who included Sir John Falconer and H. Harvey Wood as well as Sir Rudolph Bing — was justified (and Sir Thomas Beecham's prophesy of a 'perfect fiasco' confounded) it became clear that the Royal Lyceum Theatre was one of the Festival's most important assets. When Robert Ponsonby, the Festival's third director, decided in 1960 to introduce a late-night satirical revue in the official programme in order to prevent the Festival from taking itself too seriously, it is significant that the Lyceum was the theatre in which he chose to do it. To borrow a memorable phrase from George Bruce, Ponsonby wanted 'to make fun of the art at the heart of the Festival' and where better to do that than at the Lyceum? As a result of Ponsonby's decision, the international careers of Jonathan Miller, Alan Bennett, Peter Cook and Dudley Moore were launched from the Lyceum stage in a show called *Beyond the Fringe*.

If the Lyceum has been good for the Festival, however, it is equally true that the Festival has been good for the Lyceum. The prestige of being a stage for international drama — if only for three weeks a year — has added greatly to the theatre's value as a cultural asset. From 1947 onwards, any consideration of the Lyceum's history (or its future) must always include the added dimension of its role in the Festival.

This is as important today as ever it was, but twenty years ago, it was absolutely vital. Throughout the 'fifties, in the face of the irresistible competition of television, the commercial theatre circuit, of which the Lyceum formed a part, began to disintegrate and a large number of fine old theatres were forced to close their doors. It is no exaggeration to say that the Festival saved the Lyceum from suffering a similar fate.

8　The National Drama

In this chapter the role the Lyceum played in the rising awareness of a Scottish National Drama must be examined. To return to 1949. Just before Christmas of that year, the theatre world was shattered to hear of the sudden death of A. Stewart Cruikshank. Although, at seventy years of age, he could not have been expected to remain active for many more years, the abrupt manner of his passing — he died as a result of injuries received when he was knocked down by a motorcyclist — nonetheless left a gap in British theatrical life that would be impossible for anyone else to fill. Cruikshank had been one of the last survivors of a passing age, an age in which theatre had been big business, the age that television was now bringing to an end.

Television did not, of course, destroy the theatre completely, but it led to a radical alteration of both the social function of the theatre and, indeed, the very nature of the theatrical experience itself. Unlike the previous innovations — sound broadcasting and the cinema — television led to a revolution in manners, a complete change in the way that the British public led its social life. Prior to the establishment of television, this public had gone out for its entertainment and stayed at home to socialise. Television, by bringing entertainment into the home, turned this general principle on its head, as the growth in the number of quality restaurants and more comfortable public houses would appear to testify. At the same time, in the field of drama, television's fascinating combination of broadcasting, film and theatrical actuality (most TV plays went out live in the early days of the medium) offered the viewer a quality and a variety of performance with which the commercial theatre could not hope to compete.

As if the advent of television were not enough, there were other social changes which

State Visit: Charles Tripp welcomes King Olaf of Norway to the Lyceum, while Meyer Oppenheim looks on. The occasion was the last great adventure of the Lyceum's commercial period.

compounded its effect on the theatre. In Edinburgh, for instance, the great mass of the potential audience had, during the 'twenties and 'thirties, lived more or less within walking distance of the city's theatres. This audience was made up of three basic elements: the professional middle class, their servants, and a sizeable working-class element in the poorer quarters of the city. The slum clearance programme that was initiated at the end of the Second World War removed all but a small proportion of the working classes to housing schemes on the outskirts of the city, while rising costs, improved technology and a more equitable distribution of wealth eliminated the servant class altogether. As the cost of city housing soared and motoring costs diminished in real terms, even the professional classes began to move out to dormitory towns like Penicuik, where they became suburban commuters. The West End of Edinburgh, which had once provided the Lyceum with its core audience, experienced a decline in both population and quality. In the dormitory towns and housing schemes, television became, not simply competition, but a powerful disincentive to the whole practice of theatregoing.

At the time of Cruikshank's death, these new developments were still some years away from making their full impact on theatre audiences, but the signs were there for all but the most imperceptive to see. Stewart Cruikshank Jr., who took over from his father as managing director of Howard & Wyndham Ltd., certainly saw what was happening and, under his guidance, the firm changed direction in two significant ways. Over the next twenty years, Howard & Wyndham Ltd. gradually diversified its activities, moving away from theatre into publishing and book distribution. The most immediate result of Cruikshank's death, however, was that the centre of operations moved from Edinburgh to London, where Cruikshank Jr. was based.

Wilson Barrett also saw what the future held in store. According to Robert James, he warned the members of his company about the future and, in the last few years leading up to his retiral, conducted his affairs in something of a spirit of withdrawal. After Barrett's departure in 1955, there were a number of attempts to establish another repertory company, none of which were successful. These included Whatmore Productions and the Curzon Players (which was Howard & Wyndham's second attempt to found their own repertory company), but by far the most interesting of all was a season of twelve plays which were presented under the management of the London impresario Henry Sherek.

Sherek, like Cruikshank, was one of the last of a dying breed. A theatrical businessman who acted on his instincts, he had been the man behind the success of *The Cocktail Party* in 1949.

Sherek's 1956 season was something of an experiment, involving two separate acting companies — one featuring Duncan Macrae, the other Stanley Baxter — each company playing Glasgow and Edinburgh on alternate weeks. Macrae and Baxter had the support of a strong (mainly Scottish) cast, including such names as Iain Cuthbertson, Alex MacAvoy, Nell Ballantyne, Leo Maguire, John Young, Lennox Milne, Roy Kinnear, Andrew Keir, Jean Taylor-Smith, Ian Bannen, James Grant, Clarke Tait and Marillyn Gray. However, although the season included John Dighton's *Who Goes There?* and an American comedy by Mary Chase entitled *Harvey*, the main emphasis was on Scottish Drama — and twentieth-century Scottish Drama at that. Apart from Bridie's *Mr Bolfry* and Joe Corrie's *Tullycairn*, there were plays by no fewer than five living Scottish playwrights: Robert Kemp, Donald Mackenzie, Robert MacLellan, Alexander Reid and Lennox Robinson. It was the first substantial season of Scottish Drama to have been presented at the Lyceum since the days of J. B. Howard.

The reasons for this are anything but straightforward. Although it is often said (correctly) that Scotland has little in the way of a theatrical tradition, this does not mean that such a tradition is completely non-existent. The fact is that there has never been a time when Scots did not take part in some kind of theatrical activity, either writing plays or performing on the professional stage. (In this connection it is perhaps not generally realised that two of the most influential figures in Victorian English Drama, the playwright Tom Robertson and his sister, the actress-manager Madge Kendal, were the grandchildren of William Robertson, a Scottish actor from Perth.) Moreover, this Scottish Drama, though bare enough in both quantity and quality, is not at all uniform in approach and covers a fairly wide range in terms of dramatic endeavour; the satirical comedy of Archibald Pitcairne's *The Assembly*, the colloquial lyricism of Allan Ramsay's *The Gentle Shepherd*, the douce closet plays of Joanna Baillie and the spectacular adaptations of many Scott classics by various hands provide just a few examples of the versatility of which the Scottish Drama has proved capable.

It is important to discriminate, however, between the terms 'Scottish Drama' and 'Scottish Theatre'. As Professor J. F. Arnott of Glasgow University has pointed out, the galleryite who cried out 'Whaur's yer Wullie Shakespeare nou?' at the first night of *Douglas* 'overlooked the facts that the cast was English and the play written with production by Garrick at Drury Lane in view'. Prior to 1914, there was, quite simply, no such thing as a consciously Scottish Theatre. Until that time, this was not considered to be a great deficiency in Scottish life because (as has already been mentioned in Chapter Two) there was not really a consciously English Theatre either. Under the actor-manager system, the British Theatre operated within a unified structure and it is significant that it was only after the First World War (which led, as we have seen, to the demise of the actor-manager system) that the movement towards a specifically Scottish Theatre began to gather momentum.

This movement has had two, quite separate, lines of development, neither of which has ever really come to terms with the other. The first of these is essentially theatrical, having its origins in the Repertory Movement that had been established as a result of the drama of Ibsen and Shaw. Indeed, one of the first repertory companies to be

The Scottish National Players: A truly national company, the Players toured Scotland from end to end, bringing drama to every town and village that would have them. They helped to train many Scottish actors.

established in the British Isles, the Glasgow Repertory Company, is usually recognised as being the point at which the Modern Scottish Theatre was born. Established in 1909 by an Englishman, Alfred Wareing (who had worked with Benson, Tree and one of the great pioneers of the Repertory Movement, Miss Annie Horniman), the Glasgow Repertory Theatre initially sought to emulate the achievement of the Abbey Theatre in Dublin. Operating from the Royalty Theatre in Sauchiehall Street (leased, incidentally, from Howard & Wyndham Ltd. for a sum of £80 a week), the company declared its readiness to produce 'plays national in character, written by Scottish men and women of letters',

Although the history of the Glasgow Repertory Theatre is a short one — it was destroyed by the same forces which led to the end of the actor-manager system — its achievement was substantial enough to inspire a number of other companies which were established after the First World War. Most notable of these was the Scottish National Players, whose activities between 1921 and 1947 can now be seen as constituting the true beginnings of the Scottish Theatre movement. The Players were a truly national company, touring throughout Scotland (often under canvas), bringing drama to every town and village that would have them. In addition, they played all the Scottish cities and on three separate occasions — in 1922, 1923 and 1930 — took their brand of Scottish drama to London. Among the playwrights they encouraged were John Brandane, George Reston Malloch and James Bridie, while that great director, Tyrone Guthrie, gained some early experience with them. Their most important contribution, however, was the extent to which they provided, in the absence of a College of Drama, a training ground for actors. David Hutchison, in his book *The Modern Scottish Theatre*, points out the significance of this aspect of the Players' activities.

> There can be no national drama unless there are actors geared to presenting it. Although the Players' actors were trained on largely mediocre material, that training could have been put to good use in plays of merit, as it has been since, not least on the several occasions when a Scottish cast, including many former members of the Players and the other groups such as the Curtain Theatre, presented Sir David Lyndesay's *The Three Estates* at the Edinburgh Festival. Actors like James Gibson, Grace McChlery and Jean Taylor-Smith began with the Players.

Although they employed a few professionals (mainly directors), the Scottish National Players were an amateur company who were essentially populist in their approach. Their concept of a Scottish Theatre was one which would duplicate the English Theatre in everything save language and subject matter. Coincident with their activities was a cultural development which was non-amateur, non-populist and which resisted fiercely any inclination to duplicate *anything* that the English did.

In 1922, under the editorship of a young journalist called Christopher Murray Grieve, there appeared the first issue of *Scottish Chapbook*, a new magazine devoted to the arts in

Scotland. In it, under the heading 'The Chapbook Programme', there was a manifesto:

> To report, support and stimulate, in particular, the activities of the Franco-Scottish, Scottish-Italian, and kindred Associations; the campaign of the Vernacular Circle of the London Burns Club for the revival of the Doric; the movement towards a Scots National Theatre; and the 'Northern Numbers' movement in contemporary Scottish poetry.
> To encourage and publish the work of contemporary Scottish poets and dramatists, whether in English, Gaelic or Braid Scots.
> To insist upon truer evaluations of the work of Scottish writers than are usually given in the present over-Anglicised condition of British journalism, and, in criticism, elucidate, apply, and develop the distinctively Scottish range of values.
> To bring Scottish Literature into closer touch with current European tendencies in technique and ideation.
> To cultivate 'the lovely virtue' and generally to 'meddle wi' the Thistle' and pick the figs.

This was the beginning of the Scottish Literary Renaissance, a movement whose main achievement has been to radically alter the manner in which the Scots regard their Scottishness. Whatever its shortcomings — and the movement has always had enemies enough to point those out — it is undeniably true that, socially, politically and artistically, the Renaissance created a heightening of Scottish aspiration and awareness and brought a new, and altogether more honest, appreciation of many facets of Scottish life.

The founder, catalyst and, in the early years, the sole activist of the Renaissance was Grieve himself, better known to the world at large by his pen-name, Hugh MacDiarmid. As a poet, MacDiarmid won international recognition as one of the major figures in Twentieth Century World Literature, but in Scotland he is probably best remembered as a controversialist, a man of extreme views who was continually stirring up argument and debate. Although he undoubtedly enjoyed argument for its own sake — he was always, to use a

Scots expression, a 'bonnie fechter' — there was a serious purpose behind all the controversy. In the greatest of all his poems, *A Drunk Man Looks at the Thistle*, MacDiarmid sums up his motives in two short stanzas:

> I'll hae nae hauf-way hoose, but aye be
> whaur
> Extremes meet — it's the only way I ken
> To dodge the curst conceit o' bein' right
> That damns the vast majority o' men.
> I'll bury nae heid like an ostrich's,
> Nor yet believe my cen and naething else.
> My senses may advise me, but I'll be
> Mysel' nae maitter what they tell's. . . .

The Scottish capacity for self-deception was (and, despite all MacDiarmid's efforts, remains) considerable, manifesting itself most noticeably in that romantic sentimentality that is the chief characteristic of many of the better-known forms of Scottish expression. MacDiarmid recognised this quality as having a corrupting effect on Scottish life and he fought against it relentlessly, with so much success that he attracted an enormous following among all sections of the Scottish intelligentsia. Among writers in particular, Mac-Diarmid's influence has proved so potent that it is fair to say that there is scarcely a Scottish writer active today who has not been touched by it. Even when one disagrees with MacDiarmid's opinions — and since he was a Communist, a Scottish Republican, a Douglas Social Creditist and (above all else) a passionate Anglophobe, disagreeing with him is by no means difficult — the dynamic force of his argument forces his readers, if they are going to disagree, to examine their own counter-arguments in exceptionally great detail. The end result of all MacDiarmid's writing, therefore, is to sharpen the intellect of the reader. As the Irish writer AE once put it, 'I quarrel on every page, but always keep more than I throw away.'

Although he admired their energy and dedication, MacDiarmid had no great opinion of the Scottish National Players, describing their activities in the following terms:

> Their movement as they have shaped it
> depends upon popular fancy and therefore

is not free to pursue a creative purpose. And none of the plays they have produced have represented a distinctively Scottish form, the dramatic equivalent of the *differentia* of Scots psychology. They have all been alien in form, although they have been Scottish in subject, setting and, to some extent, speech. Not being new and peculiar to Scotland, they have not demanded more than conventional production and setting.

The above extract comes from an article entitled *R. F. Pollock and The Arts of Theatre*, one of a long and extremely influential series of articles MacDiarmid wrote for the *Scottish Educational Journal* in the late 'twenties, a series which was later published under the title *Contemporary Scottish Studies*. The subject of the article, R. F. Pollock, was a man after MacDiarmid's own heart. An admirer of Stanislavsky, Pollock's vision of a Scottish Theatre was completely removed from that of the Scottish National Players. In Pollock's own words, this vision consisted of evolving 'a production technique designed to deal with the un-expressed' and, in 1932, he formed a company, the Tron Theatre, to put his ideas into action. Although all his players were amateurs, Pollock's directing method, based on painstakingly detailed study of each character in the play and conducted over an extremely long rehearsal period of anything up to three months for a single production, separated the hobbyists from those who were seriously committed to the art and inculcated in the latter a sense of professional technique. It was out of this company — and others which were, to a greater or lesser extent, various permutations of its members — that the new Scottish acting profession was born.

These two lines of development, then, would appear, for all their differences in theatrical philosophy, to have had one result in common — they were training actors. It was only after a reasonably sized body of Scottish actors was created that any further progress was possible. The fact that such progress was made is largely due to the efforts of one man — the dramatist James Bridie. Apart from his plays, Bridie made two substantial contributions to the creation of a Scottish theatre:

he founded the Glasgow Citizens' Theatre in 1945 and he played a major role in establishing the Glasgow College of Drama in 1950. Although it is the latter which has proved, in the long run, to have been most beneficial to the development of a genuinely Scottish theatre, it is the former that provides us with the best example of the difficulties facing the establishment of such an institution. These difficulties are best described by Winifred Bannister in the following passage from *James Bridie and His Theatre*:

> Bridie left Glasgow an uncomfortable legacy — a theatre which was neither one thing nor the other — an Anglo-Scottish bairn dressed in the kilt for special occasions. From season to season the composition of the company changed; it was sometimes more English than Scots, sometimes the other way round. All the producers have been non-Scots, all from the English theatre. At first the compromise of an Anglo-Scots company seemed a sensible idea, but now there is no need for it. A bi-lingual Scottish actor of a good professional standard now exists. There are no Scottish professional producers because 'Citizens' has neglected to train them, to do for the Scottish apprentices what it did for John Casson. Now that a College of Drama exists to serve Scottish theatre, there will be native producers enew a few years hence. Meanwhile, the unhappy results of overlong compromise threaten the Glasgow theatre with a loss of individuality and native vigour.

The compromise of the Citizens' (and, indeed, the nature of Bridie's entire career) represents an attempt to resolve the classic dilemma of the Scottish situation, how to accommodate the need for a distinctive Scots identity within the English-dominated reality of the British context. The Scottish National Players would appear to have wished to solve the problem through the amateur movement, by building up an audience for new Scottish plays which would ultimately lead to their acceptance in the existing professional repertoire. MacDiarmid's Renaissance Movement, on the other hand, sought a completely new initiative in Scottish Drama and argued that this could only be done by establishing a Scottish Theatre which was totally independent from the English influence. Bridie, while sympathising to some extent with both points of view, realised that, for practical purposes, neither position was really tenable, and the Citizens' had been formed in order to help satisfy both aspirations. Although the compromise had the effect — in the short term, at least — of containing the dilemma, it did not resolve it and the problem remains an intractable one within the context of Scottish Theatre today.

Up until the mid-fifties, the Lyceum management was able to view these developments with complete indifference. As a commercial theatre, everything that was seen on the Lyceum stage had to be judged by its ability to show a profit. Since the theatre's very earliest of days, successive Lyceum managements had been sensitive to Scottish sentiments, had exploited them whenever possible and were certainly not unsympathetic to the idea of a Scottish Theatre. Howard & Wyndham Ltd., however, did not see it as part of their role to help create such a theatre. As private citizens, the individual board members, particularly the Scottish ones, might regret the fact that there was no Scottish company of a professional standard to match Brandon-Thomas or Wilson Barrett, but as theatre proprietors, there was nothing they felt they could do about it. It was, quite literally, none of their business and, had anyone suggested otherwise, they simply would not have been able to understand the argument. As for the theatricals, their lack of understanding, though different in nature, was every bit as total. Both Brandon-Thomas and Wilson Barrett did what they could to encourage Scottish writers and actors, but the focus of their theatre remained essentially an English one. MacDiarmid's concept of 'the dramatic equivalent of the *differentia* of Scots psychology' would have left them clueless.

In any case, the repertory companies who occupied the Lyceum were rarely able to experiment, even in the context of English theatre. In *On Stage for Notes*, Wilson Barrett makes it clear that he would never have been able to make a profit on his Lyceum seasons alone, relying on the greater capacity of the Glasgow Alhambra for this. In addition, as mentioned in Chapter Six, the Edinburgh audience was not keen on experimentation, so if he was going to break even at the Lyceum — and this was what he usually hoped to do — the accent had to be on playing safe. The need to play safe, in fact, has often been of paramount importance throughout the Lyceum's history. It has never been a theatre where huge profits could be expected and has often owed its survival to the fact that it was part of the larger organisation of Howard & Wyndham Ltd.

By 1956, however, the conditions described at the beginning of this chapter were beginning to take effect, with the result that 'playing safe' was no longer an option. With business becoming increasingly unpredictable, every single production that was seen on the Lyceum stage had to take its chances with the available audience. The management, therefore, could no longer disclaim all responsibility towards the emerging Scottish Theatre — at least, not on the grounds of commercial viability alone — and the argument for presenting Scottish plays in 'Scotland's Theatre of Tradition' became unanswerable. Furthermore, since 1953, there had existed in Edinburgh a professional repertory company which was fully committed to the establishment of a Scottish Theatre. Under the chairmanship of the Scottish playwright Robert Kemp, the Gateway Company, operating in the Church of Scotland's theatre in Elm Row, presented a wide repertoire of plays, including many by Scottish writers such as Robert McLellan, Alexander Reid, A. D. Mackie, A. B. Paterson, T. M. Watson, Ada F. Kay, Moray McLaren, James Scotland and Kemp himself. The acting company was predominately Scottish, including such names as Tom Fleming, Lennox Milne, Roddy MacMillan and Duncan Macrae. Although it was a smaller theatre than the Lyceum and it was certainly not free from financial problems, the Gateway had, at the very least, proved that an audience for the new Scottish drama existed in Edinburgh.

This is the context in which the Sherek experiment must be seen. It was, quite simply, an attempt to investigate the commercial possibilities of a growing cultural movement. Considered simply as such, the experiment was a failure. By the mid-fifties, the commercial theatre outside of London was doomed and nothing anyone could do would be able to save it. From a cultural point of view, however, the season was not only a huge success at the time, but has since proved to have exerted an enormous influence on the development of the twentieth-century Scottish Theatre. This is largely due to a single performance which dominated the entire season and which will always live in the memory of all who were fortunate enough to witness it — Duncan Macrae's playing of the title role in Robert McLellan's *Jamie the Saxt*.

In this production, the two philosophies of Modern Scottish Drama were triumphantly united. McLellan, more than any Scottish writer before or since, created a form of drama which would have been entirely suited to the ideals of the Scottish National Players. All of his plays are written in a vital and expressive form of aggrandised Scots, full of poetic delicacy and colloquial humour, and most appeal to the emotions aroused by McLellan's fundamentally populist view of the Scottish historical themes which are the prevailing concern of his drama. Macrae, on the other hand, had been a disciple of R. F. Pollock and his membership of the Tron Theatre had left its mark on an acting style in which a sense of gesture and a detailed study of character was all-important. Added to this was Macrae's unique diction — a fascinating and extremely attractive combination of Highland and Lowland intonation — and a natural projection which ensured that Macrae immediately assumed the centre of any stage he stepped upon.

Jamie the Saxt is, without any doubt, McLellan's greatest play. An exhaustively researched study of 'the wisest fool in Christendom' in the period immediately prior to his assumption of the English throne, its dialogue and dramatic structure have been worked out with a care that is equal to its content, thereby creating a sensational impact whenever it is produced before a Scottish audience. For the practical purposes of the modern theatre, however, the play has three great drawbacks. First, the extremely large cast it requires — no fewer than twenty featured roles, plus a number of supers — makes it an extremely expensive play to produce in modern conditions. Secondly, Macrae made the part so peculiarly his own that the play cannot really be produced without an actor of similar stature — and such actors are always rare. Thirdly, lacking translation, it is inconceivable, *as things stand*, that the play could be produced by a non-Scottish company. With the best will in the world, we cannot envisage a production of *Jamie the Saxt* by an English repertory company which would be anything short of a total disaster. Since it is usually only through the repertory circuit that plays are kept alive, it is therefore not surprising that, despite the successful 1956 production, McLellan's play had to wait another twenty-six years before it was seen again.

Jamie the Saxt and a number of other plays in the Sherek season made money and one cannot help thinking that the course of Scottish theatrical history would have been changed completely had this season taken place twenty or even ten years earlier. As it was, however, such success as Sherek achieved was rendered irrelevant, due to the fact that the theatrical context in which it was made was crumbling. During the late 'fifties, the commercial theatre as it had previously been known staggered towards its inevitable death. In the last years of the decade, the Lyceum was literally scraping for its existence. Apart from the Christmas show — the perennially popular *Fol-de-Rols*, a concert party featuring such comedians as a young Leslie Crowther and, later, Denny Willis — audiences were growing smaller and smaller, with the Lyceum's future looking darker and darker.

There was one bright spot, however. For three weeks in every year, the Edinburgh Festival restored audiences to their previous high levels. Throughout the 'fifties, the Festival consolidated and developed the traditions that had been established at the Lyceum in the early years. The French connection was maintained with a return visit of the Comédie Francaise in 1954, in a production of Molière's *Le Bourgeois Gentilhomme*. The great French actress Edwige Feuilliere played in *La Dame Aux Camelias* by Dumas fils in 1955, while Madeliene Renaud and Jean-Louis Barrault, as mentioned in the previous chapter, brought Anouilh's *La Répétition, ou L'Amour Puni* to the Lyceum in 1957. Nor was English drama, classical or modern, forgotten by the Festival organisers. The Old Vic played the Lyceum in 1955 and 1959, giving performances of *Julius Caesar* and Congreve's *The Double Dealer* respectively. Henry Sherek, besides producing Eliot's two later plays, *The Confidential Clerk* (1953) and *The Elder Statesman* (1958), was also responsible for Walter Hasenclever's *Man of Distinction* (which was a huge success at the time) and a Shaw double bill, comprising *Village Wooing* and *Fanny's First Play*. There was American drama with Thornton Wilder's *The Matchmaker*, presented by H. M. Tennent in 1954, and Eugene O'Neill's *Long Day's Journey Into Night* was performed by the New Watergate Theatre Club in 1958. That same year saw the appearance of one new Irish play — the Ulster Theatre Group in Gerald McLarnon's *The Bonefire* — while the following year (1959) saw the appearance of another in Birmingham Repertory Company's production of *Cock o' Doodle Dandy* by Sean O'Casey. None of these productions achieved a house percentage of less than 70 per cent, some of them were well into the nineties, and one (T. S. Eliot's *The Elder Statesman*) played to a full house for every single night of its run.

No theatre, however, can possibly hope to justify its existence on a high season which lasts for only three weeks a year and, as the decade wore on, it became increasingly apparent that the Lyceum was no longer commercially viable. On Monday, the 10th of October 1960, the following news item appeared in the *Edinburgh Evening Dispatch,* promising 'The Lyceum Is Not For Sale':

A spokesman for Howard & Wyndham Ltd. said in London today, 'There is no truth in the rumour that we are to sell the

157

theatre. We have a Christmas show all booked up. We are definitely not selling. Howard & Wyndham firmly believe that this theatre will continue for many years ahead to play a distinguished part in the life of the city.'

It has been reported that an unknown buyer was negotiating for the purchase of the Lyceum. Hence the above denial. In city business circles no one could shed any light on the name of the mysterious buyer.

Howard & Wyndham Ltd.'s denial, with its rather hollow ring, could not disguise the fact that this rumour had substance and, in *The Scotsman* the following morning, the mystery was cleared up.

Mr Meyer Oppenheim, the well-known Edinburgh businessman and managing director of James Grant & Co. West Ltd. (Furniture), admitted last night that he was the man behind the plan to transform the site in central Edinburgh which includes the Usher Hall, the Synod Hall and the Royal Lyceum Theatre.

Mr Oppenheim's ownership of the Lyceum, which will be discussed more fully in the next chapter, lasted for just three years, during which time the theatre was run by a former Howard & Wyndham manager, Charles Tripp. A former accountant who had been involved in theatre management for more than twenty years and who knew the Lyceum audience intimately, Tripp kept the theatre ticking over during what must have been a most difficult time. Since he neither had nor believed he needed to have any production experience, his approach to theatre management was firmly in the tradition of Wyndham and Cruikshank, making it strangely appropriate that he should have played a major role in what was to be

Robert McLellan The doyen of Scots dramatists. In the 1956 production of his greatest play, 'Jamie the Saxt', the two philosophers of Modern Scottish Drama were triumphantly united.

the last great theatrical adventure of the commercial period of the Lyceum's history.

In the October of 1962, King Olaf of Norway paid a State Visit to Scotland. Since official visits by foreign heads of state are usually confined to London, this in itself was a little out of the ordinary. King Olaf, however, had spent part of the war in Scotland and it was apparently at his express wish that the usual practice was suspended. The celebrations were to include a Gala Evening at the theatre and, with this in mind, the Scottish Office sought the advice of the Scottish playwright and theatre historian, Donald Mackenzie. Mackenzie had no hesitation in suggesting *Rob Roy*, the play which William Murray had produced so often and with such great success at the old Theatre Royal in Shakespeare Square. Since it was also the play which had provided J. B. Howard with his most celebrated role, it seemed appropriate that this new production should take place at the Lyceum, so an approach was made to Meyer Oppenheim, who readily agreed to take the production on.

By any standards, it was a most extraordinary production. The script was Isack Pocock's original adaptation of Scott's novel, revised by Robert Kemp. The cast contained some of the finest talents that the Scottish Theatre can boast, a number of whom have already been mentioned in the course of this history as being connected with other companies. Archie Duncan played Rob Roy, John Cairney was Rashleigh Osbaldistone, Lennox Milne was Helen MacGregor and Callum Mill was Baillie Nicol Jarvie. Among the supporting players were James Gibson, David Steuart, Pamela Kay, Andrew Downie, Morag Forsyth, Brown Derby, Walter Carr, Christopher Page, Paul Kermack, John Young, Bryden Murdoch, Jean Taylor-Smith, Michael O'Halloran, Leslie Wright and John Toye. Besides this considerable cast, there were no fewer than twenty-two supers, playing Highlanders, soldiers, huntsmen etc. The play was directed by Gerard Slevin, with settings by Anne Carrick and Sean Kenny, fights arranged by Peter Diamond, music by Cedric Thorpe Davie, played by an orchestra and chorus conducted by Richard

Telfer, with the entire production coming under the supervision of Dennis Ramsden. The man who was ultimately responsible, not only for bringing all these people together but for ensuring that the evening of the Gala Performance went off without a hitch, was the theatre manager, Charles Tripp.

It was a daunting responsibility but one which Tripp took in his capable stride. The Lyceum, of course, had had a number of Royal visits in the past — apart from those already mentioned in Chapter Five, the Duke and Duchess of York had attended the theatre during the celebration of their Silver Jubilee in 1935, the Duchess of Kent had attended a charity performance in 1938 and King George VI and Queen Elizabeth had returned in 1946 as part of the Victory celebrations — but there had never been an evening like this before. Almost the entire Royal Family was in attendance and there was great excitement during the battle scene when they apparently split into two distinct parties — one led by the Queen, the other by the Queen Mother — and stood up and cheered with all their might for the Redcoats and the Highlanders respectively!

Like all great theatrical occasions, that evening was the stuff of which legends are made, and there are many stories connected with it. For instance, the cast were unable, for security purposes, to hold their dress rehearsal in the theatre, so this took place instead in Croall's Garage, a property which Meyer Oppenheim had acquired in connection with his plan for central Edinburgh. On the night of the actual performance, interval refreshments were to have been served next door in the Usher Hall, but because of the inclement weather, Tripp arranged for those to be brought into the theatre, and the steps leading up to the dress circle sparkled with jewels and tiaras and all kinds of finery as the flower of the British aristocracy crouched on the steps to eat their cold cuts and drink their champagne. While all this was going on, Special Branch officers, ensconced in the theatre manager's office, were reportedly polishing off a bottle of whisky they had discovered there! As for the performances, these were

no less legendary. Lennox Milne made a strident, ferocious Helen, the young John Cairney a dashing Rashleigh, while Callum Mill (whose 'Doric' no doubt was every bit as 'irreproachable' as J. B. Howard's had been) scored a major success as Baillie Nicol Jarvie. Best of all, however, was the Rob of Archie Duncan, who played the part as if it had been tailor-made for him. It is not too fanciful to imagine that the ghost of J. B. Howard, who had himself struggled to overcome the difficulties he had found in the role and who had never been fully satisfied with his own performance in it, looked down on these proceedings with approval and great satisfaction.

The evening was commemorated by the publication of a quite beautiful Victorian-style souvenir programme, printed on silk. This was another idea of Donald Mackenzie's and it proved a great success. Designed by Forth Studios and printed by R. & R. Clark on silk supplied by Winterthur of Dunfermline, a copy of this programme was presented to each of the Royal guests and sold to the general public at a price of 10/- each. These programmes are now very rare, but there is one copy which can still be seen in the theatre today; it hangs on the wall in the stalls bar.

Rob Roy is usually billed as a 'national drama' and it is something of an irony that such an evening should have taken place, at the eleventh hour of its financial self-sufficiency, in a theatre which had, for most of its history, specifically rejected such a drama. This thought may well have occurred to many present at that inspiring Gala Performance, because the developments which took place over the next few years would appear to indicate that the success of *Rob Roy* could have only one logical outcome. The Lyceum had proved a worthy setting for the National Drama — did that not make it the perfect site for the creation of a Scottish National Theatre?

Put as simply as that, the proposition sounds almost absurdly simple and straightforward. The Scottish National Drama is one thing, however: a Scottish National Theatre, as we shall see, is quite another.

9   A National Theatre?

In the summer of 1960, a few months before the Lyceum was sold, the *Saltire Review* carried an article by Sinclair Shaw which put the case for a National Theatre in the most explicit terms.

> Edinburgh is rightly proud of its annual International Festival, to which it gave birth in 1947. But the glories of the Festival should not blind us to the fact that a three weeks' season is not enough, however high the standard, and to the truth that in Scotland there is no theatre where natives and visitors alike can go throughout the year to see all that is finest in the drama both of Britain and the world. Almost every state in Europe regards a magnificent national theatre in its capital as an essential part of the amenities of that city. Most European states appreciate that in the creation and maintenance of a great national theatre success is not judged by box-office results alone and realise that, like national galleries and great art galleries, national theatres deserve and must receive support from the state treasury. Edinburgh and London enjoy the unenviable distinction of being almost the only capitals in Europe without a great national playhouse, and this in an island which has produced dramatists who have never been surpassed. In Britain there is apparently a complete inability in both national and municipal circles to grasp, what in Europe is taken for granted, that national and civic theatres, if they are to fulfil their function of showing all that is best in the drama of yesterday and today must receive support from the state treasury and the civic authorities.

Shaw's article reflected the mood of the time, a mood which was conditioned by three factors: the loss of financial viability which the theatre and the performing arts generally had experienced during the 'fifties; the growing

Tom Fleming: Seen here in Brecht's 'Life of Galileo', Fleming's short reign as Artistic Director was filled with difficulty, but rich in achievement, setting out the perimeters within which the theatre could operate.

conviction that state subsidy was required for the promotion and preservation of cultural values; and, finally, a renewed sense of Scottish identity which would gain strength over the next twenty years. There is no doubt whatsoever that the call for a Scottish National Theatre and the troubled history of the attempt to secure such an institution was motivated in part by considerations of amenity and prestige rather than pure concern for the dramatic art. Quite obviously what was required was a building rather than a company. Yet, curiously enough, the fact that such efforts were made created an atmosphere in which it was possible to aim at (and, often enough, achieve) a degree of artistic success which would scarcely have been thought possible previously. In every respect, therefore, the last twenty years have seen some of the most momentous changes in the Lyceum's long history.

At the beginning of this period, of course, all the talk was of amenity. In *The Scotsman* article quoted earlier, Meyer Oppenheim was reported as having made the following statement regarding his intentions:

> If the present plans are put into effect the scheme will cost in the region of £1 million. Included in the plans are an underground car park for more than 100 vehicles, a Festival inquiry and administration offices, and a suite of conference rooms at ground-floor level which would be made available to visiting bodies.

Besides being managing director of James Grant & Co., Oppenheim was also chairman of Argyle Securities Ltd., a firm of property developers. As such, he was clearly more interested in the site rather than the existing buildings, which would obviously require to be demolished in order to carry out Oppenheim's plan. In the May of 1961, Oppenheim purchased the family business of John Croall and Sons, whose garage formed part of the same site, and it was intended that this, too, should come under the bulldozer.

Oppenheim's plan caused great alarm in the City Chambers. The loss of both the Lyceum and the Usher Hall would seriously affect the stability of the Festival — which, by this time, was contributing a sum of several millions in increased trading to Edinburgh's economy — and, even if this loss was only temporary, leading eventually to the provision of much better facilities, there was no telling what damage the absence of these key venues might do to the future of what had become an annual Edinburgh institution. The Festival apart, however, it was clearly unthinkable that such a radical redevelopment of this part of the city — a considerable section of Edinburgh's West End — should be carried out by a private property developer. Oppenheim's scheme would alter the entire character of the area, if not the city itself and, with so much at stake, the city fathers decided that they could not afford to play a passive role in this affair. Accordingly, on the 15th September 1961, it was announced by the Lord Provost, J. Greig Dunbar, that Edinburgh Corporation would buy 'the civic theatre planned for the Lyceum-Synod Hall Site' from Mr Oppenheim 'at an agreed figure' once it was built. Although the expected price was to be somewhere in the region of £700,000, this would be subject to terms negotiated between the Corporation and Mr Oppenheim. 'I would be surprised,' added the Lord Provost, 'if anything could be done within the next year.'

The negotiations, in fact, took almost two years and it wasn't until the June of 1963 that the new Lord Provost, Duncan Weatherstone, was able to announce that agreement had been reached and that the new theatre would be completed by May 1966. In the Edinburgh volume of *The Third Statistical Account of Scotland*, published in that year, Charles Graves summed up both the terms and the final outcome of that agreement.

> The Castle Terrace site was to be leased to Mr Oppenheim for 99 years at a premium of £300,000. He would then build a civic theatre which he would sell to the Corporation for about £700,000. The Lord Provost's Committee was to decide the type of theatre required, though the scheme would provide more than a theatre and result in the establishment of an art and cultural centre.

> Later, the Lyceum issue became more complicated like most issues affecting

building, streets and cultural aims in all such areas ripe for far-reaching planning schemes; and the Oppenheim scheme was abandoned. But at least, by the spring of 1964, there seemed no doubt that the Lyceum Theatre or any future theatre to be built on the Castle Terrace site would be operating as a civic enterprise on a non-profit-earning basis. The hope was also expressed by Lord Provost Duncan Weatherstone on 12th march 1964, that this civic theatre should have a first-class resident company.

The failure of the Oppenheim scheme might very easily have led to the end of the Lyceum. The Corporation took the theatre over in the spring of 1964 and it has remained in local authority hands ever since, but it should not be assumed that the city fathers had no choice in the matter. They might very easily have left the Lyceum to endure whatever fate the property market had in store for it, and, as a matter of fact, at one point it seemed that this was exactly what they would do. 'The Lyceum is a lousy theatre,' declared Duncan Weatherstone in the November of 1963, '. . . the sooner it goes over to bingo the better.' Although the Lord Provost later apologised for this ill-judged remark, the fact that he had made it in the first place appeared to signify that the Corporation were concerned solely with the site and did not regard the future of the existing building as being any of their business. The theatre was actually due to close for good on the 26th February 1964, and it was only at the very last minute that the Corporation stepped in and bought the Lyceum from Oppenheim for a price of £100,000. Quite clearly, the Corporation became involved with the Lyceum only reluctantly and would have much preferred to see the theatre in the hands of another, more suitable, owner. However reluctantly it was made, however, the Corporation's commitment to the Lyceum was an extremely unusual (and by no means universally popular) decision to take at the time and has been the source of much difficulty since. Had it not been taken, however — or had the decision gone the other way — the cultural life of both Edinburgh and Scotland would have been deprived of the contribution that

Throughout all these developments, the term 'National Theatre' was never mentioned. However, it was quite clear, from the very beginning of the Corporation's involvement, that what was being discussed was something infinitely more ambitious than a simple shoring-up of the type of theatre that the Lyceum had been over the last few years. On acquiring the theatre, the Corporation immediately formed a body to administer it. This was to be called the Edinburgh Civic Theatre Trust Ltd. and in a press release dated the 27th March 1964, the composition, objects and powers of the new body were revealed in the following plain and simple manner.

> The town council yesterday approved the setting up the new trust, which will include eight members of the council and four members from outwith the Corporation. The main objects will be to provide, maintain, improve and encourage drama, music and dance. The trust will also have powers to establish a resident group of performers which might go on tour; to arrange training for drama students; and promote a theatre club to promote an interest in the company's works.
>
> The Corporation members of the trust will be the Lord Provost, Bailie Laurence Miller, and Councillors McLaughlin, John Millar, W. Henderson, J. Kane, J. Crighton, and J. Kerr. The council authorised payment of expenses incurred in having the company incorporated, but the question of making a grant or giving a guarantee against loss was deferred.

In addition to the councillors mentioned above, three members from outwith the council joined later: the playwrights Robert Kemp and Alexander Reid, and J. B. Rankine of the Bank of Scotland. This left one vacant seat on the board, the Lyceum has been able to make over the last twenty years and would have been that much poorer for the loss. Whatever criticism can be made of the Corporation and subsequent local authorities — and over the last two decades there has been plenty — the Edinburgh city fathers saved the Royal Lyceum Theatre and they should be given credit for that.

a state of affairs which prompted much lively debate in the correspondence columns of *The Scotsman*. (In this connection, it is interesting to note that one of the participants in this debate was the Scottish Organiser of Actors Equity, Ruari McNeill, now general manager of the Royal Lyceum Company.) Nine members were deemed to be sufficient, however, and the seat remained vacant meantime.

These three non-corporation members of the Trust had all had strong connections with the Gateway Theatre Company, which was about to be disbanded after twelve extremely creative seasons of repertory. When, in February 1965, the Trust appointed Tom Fleming (who, as actor, director and on at least one occasion, author, had had similar connections with the Gateway) there were many people in Edinburgh who thought that his new company would simply be a revived version of the Gateway company, performing in more substantial surroundings. Fleming's ideas, however, went far beyond that: he was a man who had caught the mood of the time and who had both the courage and the opportunity to put it to the test. In a speech that he made to the patrons of Pitlochry Festival Theatre at the end of that July, he described his approach to the new venture with frankness and enthusiasm.

> Two questions being asked at the moment are: Is there any evidence that Edinburgh wants a civic theatre, and is there any evidence that Edinburgh needs a civic theatre?
> It is anyone's guess about the first, but I am utterly convinced about the second, because Edinburgh is not only a capital city, but a European capital city associated in people's minds with international performances of the Arts through its famous Festival.
> I am not a person who deals in much with forecasting the future; in fact, it would be fatal for me to blow trumpets and say lots of marvellous things are going to happen at the Royal Lyceum. The reason why I accepted the job in the first place is because I have always been concerned about the lack of such a theatre in Edinburgh. . . . I

hope we will be able to present theatre to people who will come to it with open minds and leave the Royal Lyceum moved to laughter for the most part, or to tears (for the right reasons, of course!) and sometimes a little baffled (not by obscurity) but by what significance a particular play has had for them.

It is not my job to say to the public what it ought to see nor to try to give it what it wants, but to present 'Total Theatre' in repertoire.

Fleming's use of the phrase 'total theatre' is both interesting and revealing. The term itself is a French one, coined by the director Antonin Artaud — broadly speaking, it means a form of theatre, which appeals to all the senses and emotions rather than simply the intellect — and, by using it, Fleming revealed his European consciousness. Quite clearly, the theatre that he had in mind was one which, while rooted firmly in Scotland, would never fail to exhibit an international awareness. In both respects, this signified an abrupt departure from the kind of theatre to which Lyceum audiences had previously been accustomed and, as such, was a policy which was full of danger. As an Edinburgh man, born and bred, Tom Fleming was well aware of this danger. In a press interview that he gave shortly before the opening of his first season, he expressed the view that his policy would either work right away or not at all. In the event, however, matters were not nearly as cut-and-dried as this.

The new company began operations immediately after the 1965 Festival.

Four plays were presented in the first season: *The Servant o' Twa Maisters*, a Scots version by Victor Carin of Goldini's classic Italian farce; a double bill by the Polish playwright Slavomir Mrozek, *Police* and *Out at Sea*; an entertainment by the Scottish poet and broadcaster George Bruce entitled *To Scotland With Rhubarb*; and, finally, Brecht's *The Life of Galileo* in which Tom Fleming played the leading role himself. These four plays ran in the theatre for ten weeks from October 1st until December 11th, a total of seventy-one performances in all.

Prior to the opening, there was a great deal of goodwill towards the new company and all the omens seemed good for a successful first season. The world-famous stage designer Abd'Elkader Farrah had turned down a number of lucrative and prestigious offers to join Tom Fleming as the Lyceum's Head of Design, and the distinguished Polish director Jan Kott had agreed to guest with the company to direct the Mrozek double bill. The new venture had caught the imagination of many people in the theatre, both in Scotland and elsewhere, and the season opened amid a great deal of excitement and eager anticipation. This atmosphere can perhaps be best described by a curious incident which took place in the theatre just three months before the start of that season.

In preparation for the opening, the Lyceum was closed for four months, during which the auditorium was given something of a facelift. This was fairly superficial, just a general tidying up, with seats and carpets being either repaired or replaced, walls and paintwork cleaned up and retouched with the odd lick of paint. In the course of this exercise, the workmen made a fascinating discovery. Just above the proscenium, hidden by the stains of decades of tobacco smoke, was the painting *Apollo and the Muses*, painted by Ballard of Paris for the Lyceum's opening in 1883. The discovery and restoration of this painting seemed to sum up and crystallize all the hopes and aspirations of the time. Just as this forgotten work of art had been rediscovered above the stage, so too, it

172

was hoped, would the heritage of Sir Henry Irving and the other great names be reclaimed upon it.

When the season eventually opened with *The Servant o' Twa Maisters* on Friday, 1st October 1965, this optimism appeared to be confirmed. The play was given a warm and enthusiastic reception, with Russell Hunter scoring a major personal success in the leading role. At the end of the performance the Lord Provost, Sir Duncan Weatherstone, made a speech in which he welcomed the new company and pledged the city's continued support. As the audience left the theatre that night, it seemed as if the best possible start had been made.

Within a month, however, the company were in deep trouble. Before October was out, Allen Wright, drama critic of *The Scotsman* and always a great champion of the civic and national aspirations of the Lyceum, was writing about the company in the most anguished tones:

> Those who care about those things must ensure that these words of Brecht's shall never apply to Tom Fleming. 'Terrible is the disappointment when men discover that their age — the new age — has not yet arrived. Then, things are not as bad as before, but much worse.'

The Civic Theatre, it seemed, was proving most unpopular with the Lyceum audience. The plays were obscure and lacked entertainment value, the seat prices were far too high and the acting company contained no 'star names'. As a result of these strictures, house percentages fell to abysmally low levels, the Lyceum became enshrouded in controversy and by the following March, there was a serious financial crisis. James Drawbell, the distinguished Scottish journalist who had temporarily joined the company to help with publicity, wrote an article for the *Evening News and Dispatch* in which he suggested that 'the time may be right for a long, cool assessment'.

While acknowledging the value of Drawbell's article as a source, this suggestion must be disputed. Six months into the life of any undertaking is altogether too soon to make this kind of assessment and it is only with the perspective of history that we are able to perceive the achievements and shortcomings of that first season.

Whatever criticisms there may have been at the time regarding plays or prices or actors, it is quite obvious to us now that the true source of the public's discontent was the repertory system that Fleming introduced. This, of course, was repertory in the original, continental sense of the word, as described in Chapter Five. It was a concept which was enjoying something of a revival at the time — several English companies had been experimenting with it — and, for practical purposes, it is a system in which there is much to be recommended. Restricting the number of plays produced saves both rehearsal time and material resources, while presenting plays on different nights of the week can lead, with the passing of time and the gaining of experience, to a maximising of the potential audience. The true repertory system, moreover, allows for a much wider range of drama to be presented, the theory being that the popular items in the repertoire will lend support to other, less popular but no less worthwhile productions. The great appeal of the system, however, is that it allows the best productions to be preserved. The production of any play is always an ephemeral affair, but a production by a regular company of players operating successfully within a system of true repertory must inevitably enjoy a much longer life.

True repertory, no less than the more familiar weekly repertory, needs time to become established — and time was the one commodity that Tom Fleming's Lyceum company just did not have. When the Corporation had taken over the theatre and made their commitment to the establishment of a resident company, it had done so on the basis of a 'twelve month trial period'. For the extremely conservative Lyceum audience — many of whom had memories of Wilson Barrett's weekly change of programme — the new system was no doubt strange and difficult to adjust to, but there simply was not the time to break them in gently. Indeed, had Fleming tried to do so — by pursuing a much less adventurous policy, for instance — the end result would probably have been no different. The irony of the matter was that, the measures which had been taken to make the best use of available resources were seen as examples of the company's subsidised extravagance, as they were not given enough time to demonstrate their effect.

Another irony lies in the fact that, of the four plays presented, three were extremely successful productions which were warmly received by all who saw them. The sole failure was the Mrozek double bill, described by Drawbell as 'little short of disastrous'. Had this been presented as part of a true repertory which had become firmly established in the theatre, it would have been carried by the other items in the bill. As it was, the effect was exactly the opposite. Far from being supported by the other plays, *Police/Out at Sea* not only nullified the impact that *The Servant o' Twa Maisters* had made, but was largely responsible for creating the image of an obscure and unentertaining repertoire. Since all other criticisms had their origin in this image, we can now see how close Fleming came to making the first season a triumphant success. As it was, the impression one receives from oral tradition is that the first season was one of unmitigated disaster.

This, of course, is quite untrue. During the short time in which Tom Fleming was Artistic Director of the Royal Lyceum Company, there were a number of substantial box-office successes

Royal Visit: Tom Fleming introduces members of the 'Galileo' cast to H.M. The Queen on the Lyceum stage.

— and the first of them took place during that first season. The following July, when H.M. the Queen, accompanied by H.R.H. the Duke of Edinburgh, paid yet another visit to the Lyceum, the play that they saw was *The Life of Galileo*, which had first been performed in the theatre the previous December. On that occasion, as James Drawbell put it, the play 'probably attracted more people than all the others put together' and had been an immediate triumph, commercially as well as artistically. On the occasion of the Royal visit, the *Evening News and Dispatch* described the performance as follows:

> It is a production which has grown in stature even from that high standard established in its first appearance. Tom Fleming's portrayal of a man whose discoveries shake accepted patterns of life to their roots, is a masterly one. Galileo is a scientist whose studies of 'the heavens' through his newly invented telescope reveal that the celestial bodies are not all that the Church of Rome has maintained them to be. Peter Dews gets the most out of his set, and his players, with Martin Heller making a welcome return to the Grindlay Street theatre as the fussing curator of the museum. Callum Mill is there, too, to add stature to the performances, as are George Cormack, the lens grinder, and Fulton Mackay as Pope Urban VIII. Eileen McCallum as the daughter caught in the web of circumstance imbues a difficult role with tremendous sympathy and understanding.

The Royal visitors, who went backstage after the performance to personally thank the cast, were delighted with the evening, even if the Duke of Edinburgh paid the Lyceum a dubious compliment by declaring that he was surprised that costumes of such quality could have been designed in an Edinburgh theatre!

The second great box-office success of the Fleming period was the company's first Christmas show, a version of the Rumplestiltskin fairy tale by David Kane. As a special attraction, a competition was organised among Edinburgh schoolchildren for the design of the costumes and

Royal Lyceum Theatre Company: The entire staff and company on stage at the beginning of the first season in 1965.

sets. This competition, which was won by nine-year-old Gordon Collins from Bruntsfield Primary School, attracted some 3,000 entries, many of which were used in the actual production. These were not simply ideas, but actual *designs*, to which Abd'Elkader Farrah did nothing more than formalise the dimensions. It must have given these children a great thrill to come to the theatre and see their designs given a practical solidity.

In the spring of 1966, the company was joined by film star Jean Kent for a production of the musical *Lock Up Your Daughters*. Directed by Peter Potter and designed by Kenneth Mellors, this show provided the Lyceum with another huge success and a rave review from the *Evening News and Dispatch:*

> The joyous escapades which the musical relates is based on Henry Fielding's comedy 'Rape Upon Rape' and provides Felix Felton with his best role to date as Squeezum, the corrupt justice who has dined not wisely but too well and who still enjoys a frolic with the ladies. His partner, whose roving eye for the gallants is no less acute, is played by Jean Kent, who scores a personal triumph in a guest appearance, showing unbounded zest which reaches hilarious heights in her rendering of 'When Does the Ravishing Begin?'. Morag Forsyth, the company's leading lady, is no less equal to the challenge, with Neville Jason looking and sounding every inch the swashbuckling hero. Paul Chapman is there too, bidding for whatever favours are going among the fairer sex. The production is peppered with delightfully drawn characters, including those of David Kincaid as the Constable; George Cormack as Politic, with a coffee house mania for newspaper reading; David Macmillan as Quill, the doddering old clerk; and Brian Cox, who shares Politic's passion for papers. . . .

Besides these successful productions, another important development which took place during Fleming's time was the formation of the Royal Lyceum Theatre Club. An inaugural meeting of the club was attended by 350 people on the 3rd July 1966. Professor K. J. Fielding of the Saintsbury Chair of English Literature at Edinburgh

University was elected the club's first chairman, subscriptions set at 10/- per annum (with students and pensioners being granted a concessionary rate of 5/-) and a figure of 3,000 was determined as the target for the eventual membership. Although this figure has never been reached — at its highest point, the membership was no more than a thousand — the Theatre Club has always been an active and well-run organisation, providing its members with a lively programme of talks, performances, theatre visits and social gatherings of all kinds throughout the year. As such, the club not only fosters an interest in theatre among the Edinburgh public, but gives the management a very useful point of contact with its potential audience.

The sensibilities of this audience were, of course, crucially important to the new company. Although Fleming had stated on several occasions that he was aiming for international recognition in advance of local acceptance, this did not mean that he discounted popular support altogether. There was a sense, indeed, in which the one form of recognition was dependent on the other. The Corporation had not saved the Lyceum simply to support the dwindling audiences of the last days of the Howard & Wyndham era, nor had the company been formed as another attempt to fill the gap that had been left by Wilson Barrett. Public subsidy, by its very nature, does not require justification in commercial terms, but it does require a tangible justification of some kind. In the case of the Royal Lyceum Theatre Company of Edinburgh, this involved a degree of national and international recognition. If this could be gained, the Edinburgh public would find the level of public subsidy completely acceptable, would be able to take pride in their civic theatre and would, as a consequence, support the Lyceum in ever-increasing numbers. This, at least, would appear to have been the theory.

The company were given their first real opportunity to put this theory into practice at the Edinburgh Festival of 1966. A critical success in the context of this great international showcase would establish the Lyceum's artistic credentials

Overleaf
The Burdies: Duncan Macrae and Fulton Mackay in Douglas Young's translation from Aristophanes. Both play and production created much controversy, dividing the critics and leading to heated debate.

181

beyond any doubt. It can be safely assumed, therefore, that the play for this first Festival offering was chosen and produced with a degree of care and a level of commitment that was even greater than usual. The result was *The Burdies* by Aristophanes in a Scots translation by Douglas Young, directed by Tom Fleming and designed by Abd'Elkader Farrah, with music by James Porter.

Douglas Young, who died in 1973, was one of the most colourful and accomplished figures in MacDiarmid's Scottish Renaissance Movement. Poet, political activist, teacher and essayist, he was, above all else, a classicist whose translations from the Greek had already won high praise. His translation of the Aristophanes comedy had originally been written for a student company (Young taught at St Andrews) and had, in fact, been produced on the Festival Fringe a few years previously. Neither the play nor the translator, therefore, could be described as an unknown quantity and, in the Lyceum, the play was given a production by a company that was uniquely equipped to do it justice. All the ingredients were present for the staging of a major Festival event.

Such an event certainly took place. *The Burdies* became one of the most controversial and talked about productions that the Festival has ever known, attracting a wide range of critical response. Young later collected all the reviews and analysed them under various headings in a booklet entitled *Scots Burds and Edinburgh Reviewers*. A random dip into this booklet gives some impression of the atmosphere that *The Burdies* created.

> . . . a riot of festive colour and humour, a peacock of a play that parades itself with glee . . .
> *Daily Record*
> As bores go, this one is positively artesian . . . director Tom Fleming's idea of a lark is my idea of a dead duck. It looks a mess, it sounds a mess, it is a mess.
> *Scottish Daily Mail*
> A brilliant production, visually and musically . . . movement on the stage is continuously exciting and amusing. Music, sets, costumes, dance and songs all share a common sense of fun.
> *Sun*

The transposition from Athens to
Edinburgh seems to me entirely successful.
. . . One is moving amongst familiar things;
the play seems immediate and real, not a
revival of something dead long ago. The
puns were outrageous, but that is just what
puns ought to be. The more general
modern references also are very successful.
. . . The whole entertainment was an
interesting bridging of the gulf between
ancient Greece and modern Scotland.
Harold Hobson *B.B.C. Arts Review*

. . . just a festival extravaganza . . . it was
neither very amusing nor (in the passages I
could interpret) very witty. A first
Edinburgh audience, untroubled by the
alarmingly braid Scots, laughed amiably at
the thickets of local allusion. . . .
Illustrated London News

The Birds turns most readily and happily to
Scots language and circumstance; and
classicists will surely agree that this
exceedingly gay, irreverent, gaudy and
melodious version is a faithful realisation of
the original script.
Glasgow Herald

A wondrous flight of fancy, *The Burdies*,
swooped over the chimney pots of Auld
Reekie last night to land slap on target.
Evening News and Dispatch

I had hoped for more than a carnival to
celebrate the fact that Edinburgh had a
civic theatre company. . . . A sense of pride
that Edinburgh could reach such heights of
stage design was tempered by the shame of
watching the Scots again present themselves
to the world as quaint, uncouth clowns,
with a pawky sense of humour.
The Scotsman

. . . a lively start . . . an agreeable show.
. . . The costumes and decorations, most
important in a production of this kind, are
in the hands of the Algerian designer
Abd'Elkader Farrah, who has suggested
with subtle skill the out-of-this-world
atmosphere on which this play depends.
Tom Fleming directs, and is to be
congratulated on an achievement.
Daily Telegraph

(The new Lyceum company's) first festival
offering is a disastrous compromise between
the demands of internationalism and the
home market.
The Observer

Reading through those reviews, one cannot help but recall a previous Festival production at the Lyceum by a Scottish company and comparing the critical reception that that was given with *The Burdies*. Sixteen years previously, as described in Chapter Seven, James Bridie's *The Queen's Comedy* (a play and production which *The Burdies* resembled in many respects) had divided the critics just as completely. There is an interestingly subtle difference, however, between the reviews of 1950 and 1966. On the earlier occasion, the unfavourable reviews had been almost wholly English in origin, while the Scottish press were practically unanimous in their praise of Bridie's play. This is always to be expected: English reviewers, confronted by a Scottish play, usually experience a feeling of alienation, 'a sense of being left out' as Harold Hobson put it, creating in them an immediate hostility which inevitably colours their judgement. On the other hand, Scottish reviewers often feel a certain pressure to wave the flag. In the case of *The Burdies*, however, this cross-border split was not at all in evidence, the polarisation of opinions moving across all sections of the press. In this respect, the critical reaction that *The Burdies* provoked was entirely typical of the kind of reception which is reserved for a theatrical event of international significance. The Royal Lyceum Theatre Company, therefore, had fully justified its existence, and the fact that this had been achieved in less than a year held out great promise for the company's future.

This future, however, would not include Tom Fleming — at least, not as artistic director. By the time *The Burdies* reached the stage, Fleming had already resigned as a result of a disagreement between himself and the board of the Edinburgh Civic Theatre Trust. Although this is not the place to discuss the rights and wrongs of that disagreement, the source of it does reveal one of the basic shortcomings of the subsidised theatre. In the old commercial days, the men who ran the Lyceum were judged simply by their ability to make a profit by attracting as large an audience as possible. The criteria by which an artistic director is judged, however, is much more diffuse, while the extent of his success or failure is much more open to interpretation. Whatever artistic success Fleming had achieved, the fact remained that, after the first year the company had made a net loss (after Corporation and Arts Council subsidies had been taken into account) of £13,245. Since all of Tom Fleming's calculations of estimated expenditure had proved to be accurate, this loss was directly attributable to loss of box-office revenue. An argument could have been made — perhaps should have been made — that this was only to be expected after such a short time and that the company needed a longer period in which to establish itself with the Edinburgh public. Tom Fleming, who had done everything that could be expected of him, was certainly not to be blamed for the financial position. The board felt, however, that his play policy in future should come under the scrutiny of a sub-committee which included the playwrights Robert Kemp and Alexander Reid. Fleming saw this as an interference with his function and resigned.

It was a tragic loss. Apart from his considerable qualities as a man of the theatre, his personal charisma had attracted many other talents to the Lyceum: Abd'Elkader Farrah, Michael Halifax (one of the most accomplished administrators in the theatre today), James Drawbell, Peter Potter, not to mention the many acting talents in the company, people like Russell Hunter, Fulton

Mackay, John Laurie, Morag Forsyth, Eileen McCallum, Una McLean and many others. In the course of a mere ten months, Tom Fleming had not only been responsible for some notable productions, but had done something which would prove, in the long term, to be even more valuable. As the first director of Edinburgh's Civic Theatre, he had, by practical demonstration, described the perimeters within which such a theatre could operate. Whoever succeeded him would be able to benefit from the experience of his mistakes while capitalising on the prestige of his success.

It must be emphasised again that at no time during this period did anyone connected with either the Lyceum or Edinburgh Corporation admit to any ambitions regarding a Scottish National Theatre. The idea, however, was in the air. Scotland, the oldest nation in Europe, began to find herself again during the 'sixties. Socially, politically, artistically and in every other way, Scots were increasingly seeing their individual ambitions in a Scottish, rather than a British context. Added to this new awareness was the fact that Edinburgh Corporation, in spite of the failure of the Oppenheim plan, remained committed in principle to the building of a multi-purpose arts complex on the site of the Synod Hall, the Usher Hall and the Lyceum. The existence of such a building might not be *called* a National Theatre, but its geographical position, at the very heart of Scotland's capital city, would be more than enough to convince visitors that a National Theatre was indeed what it was supposed to be. The Lyceum company, by virtue of its close association with the project, came to be regarded as the company most likely to occupy the new building and, as such, has had to tolerate the pressure of being judged on its suitability for this role for as long as the issue remains in doubt.

This pressure must always be taken into account whenever the Lyceum is discussed in terms of a Scottish National Theatre. Due to an unhappy combination of the ambitions of amenity and the demands of art, the term has become an extremely emotive one and there has been much misunderstanding of the Lyceum's motives in connection with it. The point really needs to be made that, even if the new building (theatre, opera house, arts complex or whatever it was to be called) had come into being, and even if the Lyceum company had taken up residence there, this fact *in itself* would not have conferred the title of National Theatre on the company. As far back as 1949, the Government had made it clear (through a statement by the Secretary of State, Arthur Woodburn) that the title of Scottish National Theatre would have to be earned. The fact that the Lyceum company has always been expected to earn it should not make us believe that there were no other candidates in the field or that the company itself has ever regarded the receipt of such a status as an eventual right.

At the same time, the Lyceum company has always been fully aware of its special position in what might be termed 'Scotland's shop window'. A great many visitors to Scotland never manage to see Perth or Dundee or even Glasgow, but they nearly all come to Edinburgh at some point during their stay. Inevitably, the impression they gain of the Scottish theatre (and, indeed, of the quality of Scottish life) is formed by what they see on the Lyceum stage. This places a very special responsibility on every aspect of the company's work in the theatre.

The Corporation's awareness of this responsibility was no doubt one of the factors which were taken into account when the Edinburgh Civic Theatre Trust was set up. Tom Fleming, too, was no less certain of what was required. In a programme note for the Royal visit of July 1966, he paid tribute to the faith and commitment of the City of Edinburgh and went on to describe what the company's response to this should be.

> The way in which we envisage most fittingly repaying a little of our debt to the city is by growing into a theatre of national significance, with a brave and restless policy and artistic standards that bear comparison with those in other European capitals.

Those words suggest struggle — and the final chapter of this history will describe the various forms that this struggle was to take.

10 'A Brave and Restless Policy'

In 1977, the Lyceum was closed for six months, during which the theatre underwent a major renovation. This was carried out on the instructions of its new owners, the Edinburgh District Council, who had taken the theatre over from the old Edinburgh Corporation at the time of the reorganisation of local government in 1975. As a result of this renovation (only the second, incidentally, that the Lyceum has received in the hundred years of its existence) the front-of-house facilities were upgraded and the auditorium refurbished and thereby creating the theatre as it stands today.

The theatre reopened on the 28th September 1977, with a Gala Performance of Ostrovsky's *Diary of a Scoundrel*, adapted by Stephen MacDonald. At this performance, which was attended by Princess Margaret, Ludovic Kennedy, chairman of the board of directors of the Royal Lyceum Theatre Company Ltd., made a speech of which the following is an extract:

> The purpose of this Gala Evening is to mark the beginning of a new chapter in the Royal Lyceum Company's history. The American civil rights leader, Martin Luther King, once said of his aspirations 'I have a dream'. Well, we have a dream too, and that is that, given the facilities we need, and only after having proved ourselves worthy of it, we shall be permitted to grow into the National Theatre of Scotland. During the past few years, there has been the birth of Scottish Opera and Scottish Ballet — but they, like their elder sister, the Scottish National Orchestra, have found their permanent homes in another place. Let us see to it that we keep our national theatre here in our capital city. We at any rate will work for that goal and we hope that you will support us.

Although Kennedy's speech was the expression of an ideal rather than a declaration of

Willie Rough: Fulton Mackay, Archie Duncan and John Cairney in Bill Bryden's first play. 'Willie Rough' set an encouraging example to a whole new generation of Scots playwrights.

policy — in this respect, it is important that his qualifications regarding facilities etc. be noted — it does give a fair indication of the mood of optimism which prevailed at the time. This optimism was anything but misplaced. Over the previous decade, the Lyceum Company had grown and developed in all manner of directions and had reached the point where it was practically the only theatre company in Scotland which could pitch its ambition at such a height of excellence.

When Tom Fleming resigned as artistic director in 1966, there was a great deal of speculation over the identity of his successor. The names of many theatrical luminaries — from Scotland and elsewhere — figured in the rumours which inevitably circulated. At the end of the day, however, it was clear that there were only three real contenders — Iain Cuthbertson, Victor Carin and a young director from Leicester called Clive Perry. The first two names were instantly recognisable to everyone in Scotland, but no one outwith theatrical circles had ever heard of the third. On the face of it, Perry seemed the darkest of dark horses. To begin with, he was an Englishman and the public expectation was that a Scot would be appointed. His lack of Scottishness, however, mattered less than his lack of prestige. He was not a famous theatrical figure whose reputation would command instant respect and, although it was known that he had successfully managed the Phoenix Theatre in Leicester, this did not mean much to the average Edinburgh theatregoer. (In point of fact, Perry's Leicester experience probably stood him in good stead: a generation earlier, Wilson Barrett had taken his company there for a season and found, to his horror, that Leicester was something of a theatrical graveyard where the local press did not even bother to carry theatre notices!) It was something of a surprise, therefore, when the announcement was made that Clive Perry had been appointed.

One of the first things that Perry did on taking over was to close off the gallery, thereby reducing the Lyceum's capacity (1,647 seats in 1966) to manageable proportions. He also reduced seat prices and introduced a play policy in which first-class contemporary drama, the classics and popular comedies were all given their appropriate place. 'Theatre is not pure art,' Perry told Allen Wright in a press interview in 1968. 'It is the art of compromise in many ways. You can only produce what the public want, and not force undesirable commodities down their throats.'

It might have been F. W. P. Wyndham speaking. As a man of the theatre, indeed, Clive Perry bears a strong resemblance to both of the Lyceum's founders. Like Wyndham, he is a competent actor (although he rarely performs) and a talented director (particularly of comedy) whose true forte is nevertheless a certain gift for management. Rather less noticeably, however, he resembles Howard in that, during his time at the Lyceum, he conducted the theatre's affairs with a high degree of enthusiasm and flair. It was Perry, for instance, who rediscovered and reinstated the two carved wooden figures that had once occupied prominent positions in the Lyceum foyer. These comically grotesque figures, nicknamed 'Howard' and 'Wyndham' by a previous generation of actors, are cartoon-like representations of rural bird-catchers which had been gifted to the theatre when it was built. According to tradition, they originally belonged to Sir Walter Scott and had been part of the furnishings of his house at Abbotsford. Perry found them in an attic, had them cleaned and restored and put them back on display. They can now be seen at the entrance to the stalls bar.

The restoration of these figures, of course, attracted a certain amount of publicity and this was another area in which Perry displayed a high degree of expertise. His first production, for instance, was Shaw's *The Devil's Disciple*, in which the leading role was taken by Bryan Marshall. At the time, Marshall was appearing twice-weekly in *United*, a popular television series about a football team. Press coverage of the time reveals that there could be few people in Edinburgh who were not aware of the fact that this television favourite could be seen in the flesh at the Lyceum. It was due to tactics such as this that Perry was able, in his first year, to cut the Lyceum's deficit in half and to wipe

it out altogether by the following year.

At the same time, the high artistic standards which had been both the aim and the achievement of Tom Fleming's company were not forgotten. In an interview with John Cribbin of the *Evening News and Dispatch*, he paid tribute to his predecessor:

> The point about Tom is that he started when the Lyceum as a civic theatre was a brand new venture — and as far as I am concerned that is by no means an easy business in a city like Edinburgh. He paved the way and as far as I am concerned it was the right way in most respects. I am now just following out his policy with a few variations.

This, of course, was the right thing to say — Perry always knew the right thing to say — but it was also very true. To no lesser extent than Tom Fleming, Perry believed in a 'brave and restless policy' for the Lyceum and put his belief into practice from the very start. Although he tended to direct the more commercial productions himself — this was his forte — he gave his associate directors a great deal of scope to produce contemporary drama of the highest quality on the Lyceum stage.

Among those associate directors, the name which immediately leaps to mind is that of Richard Eyre. Another Englishman, Eyre's association with Perry began in Leicester in 1965 when he had persuaded Perry to allow him to produce a Sunday night production of Ann Jellicoe's *The Knack*. The success of this production began an extremely creative relationship which was to last until Eyre finally left the Lyceum in 1972. During these seven years, Eyre was responsible for so many quality productions that any fully comprehensive assessment of his work at the Lyceum is quite impossible in the available space. A few examples, however, will give some indication of the versatility and skill of this talented director.

In his first year alone, Eyre directed an astonishingly wide range of drama, his productions including Chekhov's *The Seagull*, O'Casey's *Juno and the Paycock*, McLellan's *The Hypocrite*, David Halliwell's *Little Malcolm and his Struggle with the Eunuchs*, and John McGrath's *Events While Guarding the Bofors Gun*. Perhaps the most notable of his earlier successes, however, was his own adpatation of Jennifer Dawson's novel *The Ha-Ha*. Although this novel had been a great success when it was first published in 1961, winning the James Tait Black Memorial Prize for that year, Jennifer Dawson had resisted all previous attempts to dramatise the story, turning down several lucrative offers for the stage and screen rights. Eyre's determination, however, had been so great that he

The Hypocrite: McLellan's last play at the Lyceum in 1967. It was not, however, his last production. 'The Flooers o' Edinburgh' was revived by Bill Bryden in 1976.

had written the play without any prior permission whatsoever. When he had sent his script to the author for her approval, this was not immediately forthcoming, but Jennifer Dawson was interested enough to work with Eyre on the stage version which was eventually seen at the Lyceum. In his direction of the play, Eyre not only drew a fine performance from Angela Pleasence, but an equally fine piece of reviewing from Allen Wright.

> . . . Angela Pleasence gave a brilliant performance as a distracted patient. The psychiatrists and nurses cannot penetrate the wall around her — in a sense this is the 'ha-ha' of the title — but a fellow-patient establishes a fleeting relationship. This encounter with Alasdair creates havoc with her vulnerable nature, but it makes her more aware of herself and the joy within her. . . .
> She is another Alice, alarmed and even amused by the wonderland that society tries to organise and diminish. If Richard Eyre has made an excellent job of translating the novel into dramatic form, he has been greatly assisted by Angela Pleasence. Surely no other actress could play this part so perfectly — a still, small, huddled figure with deep-set eyes and a frown conveying infinite preoccupation. Strands of hair fall over her face, whose blankness occasionally lights up, just as her gentle voice can be suddenly roused to passion.

In complete contast to *The Ha-Ha* were the Christmas shows that Eyre directed at the Lyceum. The first of these, a spectacular version of Stevenson's *Treasure Island*, was somewhat marred by the fact that Duncan Macrae, who was to have played Long John Silver, had to leave the production as a result of an illness which turned out to be his last. (He was replaced in the production by Russell Hunter, but he has never been replaced in the Scottish theatre by anyone — and probably never will be.) Somewhat happier memories are evoked of the following year's Christmas show, in which Dickens' *A Christmas Carol* was given a similar treatment. In this production, two old favourites from the Wilson Barrett days returned to the Lyceum — Walter Carr played Scrooge, while

Donald Layne-Smith appeared as Marley's Ghost. The music was composed by David Dorward and the entire enterprise added up to the kind of sensation which had the critics raving. Allen Wright's piece was fairly typical:

> Richard Eyre, David Dorward and Walter Carr have concocted a grand bowl of punch, strictly according to the recipe devised by Dickens. It could hardly fail to bring a glow of goodwill to the most crabbed countenance. The flavour is sweet but the effect is stimulating. Richard Eyre's skilful adaptation of the story retains the hard streak of reality behind the rosy glow of benevolence — the melancholy social comment that underlies the merriment. We can't help feeling that Scrooge's conversion is more fanciful than the bleak vision revealed to him by the spirit of the future. But this is the season of the year for banishing grim spectres, and so happiness prevails.

When the Corporation appointed Clive Perry Director of Edinburgh Theatres in 1970, giving him responsibility for the King's as well as the Lyceum, Eyre was appointed Director of Productions and it was in this capacity that he took the Lyceum company on tours of West Africa (1971) and the Far East (1972). He directed Thomas Middleton's *The Changeling* and a version (by Jack Ronder) of Hogg's *Confessions of a Justified Sinner* at the 1970 Festival, and won production awards from Scottish Television on the three consecutive years from 1969 to 1971. He will probably always be remembered in Edinburgh, however, as a superb interpreter of Chekhov, his 1968 production of *Three Sisters* providing an excellent example of this aspect of his work. Allen Wright, who once suggested that the Edinburgh Festival mount a Chekhov season and engage Eyre to direct it, welcomed the 1968 production thoughtfully.

> Happiness eludes these people but that does not mean that it is a gloomy play. The bleakness of their existence in a provincial garrison town is relieved by kindness and humour which Mr Eyre gently emphasises. Many of the characters behave absurdly but they are all pitiful — even the awful

Natasha who swamps the household with her vulgarity. The high level of all the performances makes us just as interested in the plight of the foolish schoolmaster, or the jealous Soliony, as in that of the three sisters themselves. The company seemed a little uneasy in the cheerful first act, conserving their emotions for the rest of the play. The variations in mood were managed superbly — gaiety quenched or grief softened in a moment by a sudden change of key. In repose or in almost speechless hysteria, Angela Pleasence was always touching and delicate as Irena. The oldest sister, Olga, was given an impressively maternal quality by Antonia Pemberton — protective and sympathetic. Elizabeth MacLennan was subdued and poignant as Masha, enraptured by Vershinin . . . played admirably by Alan Brown. Katherine Barker's Natasha had all the petulance of someone nursing an inferiority complex.

Apart from his productions, Eyre made a substantial contribution to the life of the Lyceum by opening the theatre up to all sorts of other activities. Drama conferences, folk concerts, large-scale poetry readings (organised by the poet Alan Bold) are just three examples of the kind of occasion which was promoted in the theatre under Eyre's influence. Not the least of these activities was the Young Playgoers Club, organised by Michael Burrell, Sue Birtwistle and (later) Brian Stanyon. In the spring of 1967, the Young Playgoers Club presented an 'all our own work evening', in which the four youngest read a selection of Scots poetry, while the others performed three short plays which they had written and directed themselves. The most successful of these was deemed to be *Parochial and Perspectful*, by two pupils of George Watson's College, Stephen Fox and William Pryde. Pryde later became a trainee director at the Lyceum — he is, at the present time of writing, director of the Cambridge Theatre Company — during which time he helped make an important contribution to the work of the company. The youth policy, initiated by Tom Fleming's production of *Rumpelstiltskin* in 1965, was continued under Perry.

Youth was also to be encouraged in

the audience. During the 'fifties and 'sixties, a new form of theatre had begun to emerge which had a predominantly young audience. Since this new form had been given considerable impetus by the existence of a plethora of unofficial appearances at the Edinburgh Festival, the term 'Fringe Theatre' has been coined to describe it. The Edinburgh connection, too, has led to the city becoming something of a centre for Fringe Theatre, with two new theatres of this type — the Traverse and the Pool — being established in the 'sixties. Cosmopolitan in its appeal, intimate in its performance, Fringe Theatre usually contains a high degree of radical social commitment and aesthetic awareness in the themes of its repertoire, making it very popular among the thousands of young people who throng the city from all over the world during the summer months, not to mention the resident student population. The Lyceum has always been keen to serve this audience. In an article for the *Evening News and Dispatch* in 1967, one of the board members, the Scottish playwright Alexander Reid, touched on this aspect of the company's work.

> One of Mr Perry's long-term hopes is that Edinburgh will one day, in addition to its main theatre, have a smaller auxiliary house where, at modest levels of presentation, important and new plays which are believed, for the time being, to be too risky for inclusion in the main theatre programme, could be given try-out productions. Perhaps Mr Perry's hope will be realised when Edinburgh's new Arts Centre on the Synod Hall site is eventually constructed.

Mr Perry's hope, however, was not prepared to wait that long and five years later the second auditorium was in existence. This came about as a result of the creation of the Young Lyceum Company, a short-lived but vitally creative and extremely popular initiative that the Lyceum made in the field of Fringe Theatre. Originally formed in 1972, the Young Lyceum's first performance took place not at the Lyceum but at the Netherbow (the new theatre that the Church of Scotland built with the proceeds from the sale of the Gateway) when a double bill comprising Beckett's

Endgame and Stoppard's *The Real Inspector Hound*
was presented. Three years later, in 1975, the
company took over an old Festival booking office
in Cambridge Street, next door to the main
building, and by dint of their own efforts
transformed it into an excellent studio theatre with
a capacity of 200 seats.

Under the leadership of actor/
directors Ian Ireland, Billy Pryde and Peter
Farrago, the Young Lyceum generated tremendous
energy and displayed such a high level of commitment that it attracted the very brightest of the
emerging talents in the Scottish theatre. These
included (among others) the actors Martin Black,
Ronnie Letham, Tom Marshall, Bill Paterson,
Libba Davies, Deborah Fallender, Maggie Jordan
and Ann Scott-Jones; the musicians David
McNiven and Angie Rew; choreographers Stuart
Hopps and Pat Lovett; and the actor/playwrights
John Bett and Sean McCarthy. Other new young
playwrights whose work was performed by the
company included Lindsay Levy and William
Grant. They performed new versions of the classics
— including one up-dated version of *A Midsummer
Night's Dream* which they performed on Leith
Links during the 1973 Festival — a Christmas show
based on Charles Kingsley's *The Water Babies* and,
of course, much new work, including two musicals
— *Aimee* (based on the life and times of Aimee
Semple McPherson) by Lindsay Levy, and *Cry
Wolf* by Sean McCarthy and David McNiven. The
Young Lyceum also appeared on the official
Festival with a production of Buchner's *Woyzzek*.

For all its creative success, however,
the Young Lyceum was inevitably a very expensive
venture and Clive Perry, whose publicly stated
opinion was that the theatre's business 'to live
within the income it has', needed to balance such
ventures with more commercial productions. One
of the first of these resulted in the return to
Edinburgh, after an absence of many years, of the
legendary Scots comedian Dave Willis. This
Chaplinesque clown (whom Chaplin himself had
seen and admired) appeared at the Lyceum in the
spring of 1967, playing opposite Jimmy Logan in a

production of the Broadway musical *A Funny Thing Happened on the Way to the Forum*. Perry's greatest commercial success, however, took place some eighteen months later, in the autumn of 1968. Directed by Michael Meachan and designed by Geoffrey Scott, Jay Presson Allen's adaptation of Muriel Spark's *The Prime of Miss Jean Brodie* created more public excitement — if one excludes the Festival productions — than perhaps any play since *Swords About the Cross*.

The opening night of *The Prime of Miss Jean Brodie* was a Gala Evening in aid of the Duncan Macrae Memorial Fund. As a tribute to Macrae, a poem had been commissioned from Hugh MacDiarmid which was presented as a prologue to the play. Entitled *Cranks never make good democrats*, it is not one of MacDiarmid's better poems — he was never at his best when asked to write to order — but it is much better read aloud than it seems on the page. Using the kind of excruciatingly grotesque doggerel that Macrae had excelled in presenting, the poem is nonetheless infused with the true spirit of MacDiarmid, as the last three stanzas make uncompromisingly clear:

> All the ubiquitous false Scottishness
> He alone, it seems, could expose
> With one thrust of an elbow or knee
> Turn of a bony wrist or poke of his nose.

> If ten just men sufficed
> To save a city long ago
> We may well to Duncan Macrae alone
> The salvation of the Scots genius owe.

> Most theatregoers are morons, you said,
> But why did you, dear Duncan, limit it
> To theatregoers—it's true of all here.
> There's no replacement now for your wit.

To precede a performance by informing the audience that they are all morons is not exactly the best way to get the play of the evening off to a flying start! *Miss Brodie*, however, soon proved herself more than capable of dealing with the situation, scoring a major success both critically and at the box-office. In addition to a rave review from Allen Wright, the play also won recognition from Wilfred Taylor's daily column *A Scotsman's*

Log. Discussing Edinburgh's well-worn reputation for being a 'cesspool of respectability', Taylor went on to make a point which he considered pertinent:

> If respectability is virulently epidemic in Edinburgh, the inhabitants show a healthy tendency to laugh at their symptoms when presented in lively outline. Muriel Spark's splendid play 'The Prime of Miss Jean Brodie' is currently attracting packed houses to the Royal Lyceum. There is nothing to indicate that Morningsiders, putatively the ranking puritans in town, have been conspicuous by their absence. And no one could claim that Miss Brodie in her prime was the epitome of what is considered to be Morningside respectability — even if the poor soul could not altogether divorce the respectable from the wanton in her make-up in moments of abandon with music masters at swinging Cramond.

The Prime of Miss Jean Brodie: Pekoe Ainley as Muriel Spark's heroine in Jay Presson Allen's stage version of her novel. This production was a theatrical triumph.

In the Lyceum production, the part of Miss Brodie was played by Pekoe Ainley, who 'achieved a perfect balance of the absurd and the vulnerable' according to Allen Wright. The key part of Sandy was played by Susan Macready, while the two men in Miss Brodie's life, the lecherous art master and the plodding music teacher, were played by Victor Carin and John Shedden respectively. The real laurels of the production, however, were won by Lennox Milne as the headmistress of the Marcia Blaine School for Girls, repeating in Edinburgh the part she had played with great success in the Broadway production of the play.

The theatrical triumph of *The Prime of Miss Jean Brodie* had the effect of highlighting the great deficiency in Clive Perry's artistic policy — there had been virtually no Scottish drama. The reasons for this were quite straightforward. No suitable play had been submitted to the theatre and, even if such a play had turned up, neither Perry nor Eyre, as Englishmen, would have felt competent enough to direct it. Perry's lack of competence, however, did not prevent him from having an opinion on the subject. In the 1968 interview with Allen Wright which was mentioned earlier, he accused Scottish writers of betraying the cause of modern Scottish drama by dwelling too much on historical subjects and confusing the national drama with the preservation of Lallans.

> I don't believe the public are willing to sit through a play whose vocabulary they don't understand. As regards the future of Scottish theatre, it may be that there is no such thing as a totally individual Scots language left. National drama with a tongue of its own is not for the future. Plays about contemporary Scotland will be in English with only a slight accent.

The above statement (which bears a markedly strong resemblance to dozens of similar statements regarding the Scots language over the last two hundred years) is, of course, completely fallacious and would have fallen squarely into the 'famous last words' category had it not been for the fact that Perry kept an open mind on the subject. Later in the same interview, he indicated that he had given the matter a great deal of thought by complaining of his difficulties in casting Scottish plays, brought about by the fact that most of the best Scottish actors were in great demand for television serials and, as a result, were based in London. Quite clearly, Clive Perry had no prejudices in this respect and, when the right play came along, he welcomed it.

At the beginning of the 'seventies, such a play did, in fact, come along. It was called *The Burning* and it had been written by the poet and playwright Stewart Conn. At first sight, *The Burning* bears a strong resemblance to much recent Scottish drama: it is historical in setting and subject-matter (dealing with the witchcraft trials of the reign of James VI) and its dialogue is written in a form of artificial Scots which sounds odd to modern ears. Given the exposure of a production, however, several important differences emerge between *The Burning* and the drama of McLellan, Kemp and Reid.

To begin with, *The Burning*, unlike the earlier plays, uses a non-naturalistic convention, a succession of short scenes being played on an open stage. Secondly, the narrative of the play is punctuated by songs which are sung by the King's jester (played uproariously in the original produc-

The Burning: Joseph Brady and Jeni Giffen in Stewart Conn's anti-historical drama which broke new ground in Scottish playwrighting. 'The Burning' was Bill Bryden's first Lyceum production.

tion by John Grieve) and two of his cronies. Lastly (and most importantly), the language that Conn uses is *genuinely artificial*. The form of Scots employed by the older dramatists might *seem* artificial, but it can only be described as such in the sense that this is true of *all* literary and theatrical language. The work of Robert McLellan and the others was an attempt to give a formal expression to a language which continues to be spoken by a great many people, albeit in a less aggrandised form. The strangeness and unfamiliarity of the Scots used in the earlier plays, therefore, can be seen to be incidental, being the strangeness of hearing familiar speech employed in an unfamiliar setting. In *The Burning*, Conn quite deliberately makes use of this effect — which Bertolt Brecht has described as 'the alienation effect' — to challenge his audience's perceptions and to concentrate their attention. In this respect, therefore, *The Burning* can be seen as the first attempt to apply a truly modern consciousness to the Scottish drama.

The Burning, which was produced at the Lyceum in 1971, is important for another reason, however. Perry had known about the play since 1968, but had delayed its production until he could find a suitable director. Eventually, he found the right man for the job and *The Burning* was the first Lyceum production of the Scottish playwright and director, Bill Bryden.

The impact that Bill Bryden made on Scottish drama during his few short years at the Lyceum cannot be overemphasised. As one of Perry's associate directors, he gathered about him a company of quite remarkable quality, including such names as Rikki Fulton, James Grant, Roy Hanlon, Eileen McCallum, Fulton Mackay, Roddy McMillan, Clare Richards, Jan Wilson and Paul Young. As a director, he produced a fairly broad range of drama, from a skilful treatment of Barrie's *What Every Woman Knows* to a quite beautiful presentation of O'Neill's *The Iceman Cometh*, in which Ian Bannen appeared as Hickey and that wonderful Irish actor, J. G. Devlin, played the part of Harry Hopkins. Besides being responsible for two Festival productions — John Morris's *How*

Mad Tulloch Was Taken Away in 1975 and Tom Wright's version of Sir David Lyndesay's *Ane Satire of the Thrie Estaitis* in 1976 — Bryden persuaded Roddy McMillan to write his second play, *The Bevellers* (which, sad to record, was also to be his last), and revived, with great success, Robert McLellan's satirical comedy, *The Flooers o' Edinburgh*. It was as an author, however, that Bryden was to make his most notable contribution. His first play, *Willie Rough*, not only broke completely fresh ground in the field of Scottish drama, but set an encouraging example to a whole new generation of Scottish playwrights. Partly as a result of this example, the decade of the 'seventies witnessed the greatest upsurge of native dramatic writing that Scotland has ever known.

Set during the First World War, *Willie Rough* tells the story of a Clydeside riveter and his struggle to come to terms with the times in which he lives. The plot (which is based, incidentally, on the experiences of Bryden's own grandfather) is appealing enough, but what excited audiences and critics alike was the manner of its presentation. Written as if it were a film-script — full of short, effective scenes which ripple along in perfect harmony with each other — the play is a convincingly accurate recreation of its chosen time and place. There is more to this than mere authenticity, however. In its evocation of the period, the play is clearly in touch with its audience's awareness of that period and, as such, stands up as a vital expression of a common Scottish experience.

A clear example of this can be given with reference to the language that Bryden uses in the play. On the face of it, this would appear to have nothing whatsoever in common with either the aggrandised Scots of McLellan or the artificial Scots that Conn used in *The Burning*. Aiming at authenticity, Bryden would appear to have disregarded formalisation in his careful and loving rendering of the cadences of Scottish urban working-class speech. The result of this, however, is not simply a collection of rough-hewn characters 'speaking common', but rather a carefully balanced dramatic dialogue. Towards the end of the play, for instance, there is a statement of great dignity which draws much of its power from the fact that it is spoken in the natural and logical context of a fairly ordinary conversation. Refused work in the shipyards, Willie Rough (played in the original production by James Grant) discusses his future with his friend, Pat Gatens (Joseph Brady).

> *Pat* There's other jobs forbye rivetin.
> *Willie* Aye. The Army.
> *Pat* Don't be daft. There's the farmin. They need farmers the-nou. Get out o the grime. I wish I could go tae the country.
> *Willie* I like the grime. I've got tae stay,
> *Pat* I've got tae show folk what it's like tae live by somethin' ye believe in. Mebbie I can change them by showin them that. Mebbie I cannae. But I've got tae haud my heid up, so that they can stick up for themselves an' no be feart tae demand what's theirs by rights. They can call me any name they like. They can brand me wi any slogan, any party, and I'll answer tae them aa. They can jyle me again if they want tae, an' if they throw anither brick at my heid, it had better kill me! 'Cause I'm here, an' I'm gonna haunt Jake Adams an' every worker in this river an' Cosgrave an' aa. I'll haunt them till they see sense or tae my time's spent. I'll turn everything upside doun an' backside foremost or die tryin. There's worse tae come.
> *Pat* But ye havenae got a start yet, Willie.
> *Willie* But I will, Pat. I've got tae.

Apart from its excellence as a piece of drama, there is no doubt that *Willie Rough* is a more adequate reflection of the spirit of the time in which it was written and first performed. By 1972, the rediscovery of Scottish identity which had been gathering momentum throughout the 'sixties was about to move into a completely new phase. The most dramatic manifestation of this, of course, was the return of no fewer than eleven Scottish National Party Members of Parliament to Westminster in the two General Elections of 1974. This political development, however, was not the cause of this new Scottish awareness, but had come about, rather, as a result of it. In all manner of areas, from merchant banking to scientific research, new and distinctively Scottish institutions were being set up and distinguished exiles were coming home to commit their talents to Scottish society in a spirit that transcended politics.

In the arts, of course, the re-emergence of the Scottish identity was particularly noticeable. The old Scottish Committee for the Encouragement of the Arts had evolved, by degrees, into the Scottish Arts Council, a substantial public body with a commitment, enshrined in its charter, to increase the accessibility of the arts to the general public. As a result of its activities, many areas of artistic life which might otherwise have perished have survived and, indeed, flourished. Opera, ballet, literature, concert music and film are all departments of the arts which owe their very existence in Scotland to the financial assistance that the Arts Council has been able to give them. Theatre, too, has received much in the way of Arts Council subsidy — but here the problem is rather more difficult. Unlike the afore-

Ane Satire of the Thrie Estates: The greatest Scottish play of them all, revived by Bill Bryden in 1976. Tom Wright prepared a version of Sir David Lyndesay's text.

mentioned arts, theatrical activity is so diffuse, operating on so many different levels, that the Arts Council has always been faced with a dilemma regarding the disbursal of its considerable (but limited) resources for the subsidy of Scottish theatre. This dilemma is the classic one of whether to spread financial resources thinly over a wide area — thereby giving a *little* help to a *lot* of organisations — or whether to seek greater value for money by making a greater investment in a more selective manner.

In 1970, the Scottish Arts Council began to give consideration to the idea of creating a major drama company which would not only tour larger Scottish venues but which would also tour extensively throughout the United Kingdom and abroad. A number of ways of accomplishing this were discussed, but the multi-purpose arts complex which Edinburgh Corporation were still planning to build on the Castle Terrace site was, quite obviously, a factor which figured largely in the Arts Council's deliberations. Once this building was completed, it would solve a number of the Arts council's problems at a stroke, thereby creating great economies of public expenditure on the arts. Not only would the new building be the base for the new company — tentatively given the name of the Scottish Theatre Company — but it would also provide a home for Scottish Opera and Scottish Ballet, thus creating a focal point for the performing arts in Scotland.

Accordingly, after discussions between the Arts Council and the Edinburgh Civic Theatre Trust, Clive Perry conducted a preliminary exploration of the practical problems involved in creating such a company in the new theatre. The result of this exploration was the outline of a plan — although described by Perry as a 'rough company structure' it is, in fact, much more elaborate than that name suggests — involving not one company but three, costing (at 1972 prices) a total subsidy of £200,000 which was to be met partly from Arts Council funds, partly from contributions from the Scottish local authorities. The three companies Perry envisaged were (a) the Scottish

Theatre Company that the Arts council wished to create; (b) a resident company which would perform the more popular plays and pantomimes (and which would also go on tour); finally (c) a 'young company' (based, presumably, on the work of the Young Lyceum) which would likewise tour.

Although the Arts Council did not give Perry's plan immediate endorsement, it did give the Lyceum company additional financial assistance to explore the possibilities of large-scale touring in Scotland, and it was tacitly agreed that the Lyceum should move gradually towards acquiring the status of a National Company. One can easily understand the Arts Council's caution in this respect. The entire strategy was linked directly to the completion of the new building on the Castle Terrace site and, as the years passed and endless difficulties were encountered, the prospect of this happening looked increasingly unlikely. Eventually, these difficulties proved insuperable, the project was finally abandoned, and the Arts Council had to think again about the whole subject.

The mid-seventies proved to be a time of great upheaval for the Lyceum. Clive Perry, who might have been persuaded to stay if the Castle Terrace project had gone ahead, decided that the time had come to move and left to become artistic director of Birmingham Rep. Bill Bryden, too, accepted the position of associate director at the National Theatre and left for London, as did another Perry associate, Robert Kidd (who was, however, only at the Lyceum for a brief period) when appointed co-director of the Royal Court. Coincident with these departures was the reorganisation of local government, in which Edinburgh Corporation was, in effect, abolished and replaced by the two-tier authority of Lothian Region and the Edinburgh District Council. With the disappearance of the Corporation, the Edinburgh Civic Theatre Trust was wound up and the Lyceum Theatre and its resident company became two separate entities. This is the position that obtains today, in which the Royal Lyceum Theatre Co. Ltd. pays a rent for the occupancy of the theatre to the proprietors, the Edinburgh District Council.

This new chapter in the Lyceum's history, however, cannot really be considered here. Although each of the present company's artistic directors — first Stephen MacDonald and now Leslie Lawton — has had his own individual contribution to make, the activities of both are of much too recent incidence to be viewed with any degree of historical perspective. Time, as Edmund Burke once remarked, is a 'grand instructor' and the true significance of some of the events of the past few years will only be fully understood when they can be considered from the distance of a decade or so. Already, indeed, after no more than a mere six years, the ideal expressed by Ludovic Kennedy in his speech at the 1977 Gala Performance would appear to have been overtaken by more recent developments in the Scottish Theatre.

If the substance of Kennedy's speech is dated, however, the spirit of it is not. The words he spoke in 1977 carry a strangely moving echo of some other words, spoken by J. B. Howard, on the evening of that first performance on September 10th, 1883. Since they present us with perhaps the happiest of any of the parallels that can be discerned between that time and our own, recalling them is surely the most appropriate way in which to conclude this history of the Royal Lyceum Theatre.

> This is the prologue to the chapter new
> Of our own fortunes; and the aim is true—
> To flood with rosier colours all the past,
> That boasts its thousand heroes; every age
> Is thronged with memories, braver grown
>   with years
> While rivalry with generous fire appears
> To feed the sacred flame. Proud of our
>   prize.
> Won in the fight before your very eyes,
> A brighter garland still we'd fain disclose:—
> Our own colours are the green, the rose
> Is Wyndham—while forget-me-nots entwine
> For old acquaintance sake; with trophies
>   fine
> As these, I see a vista spreading bright
> Down through the future's forest, and the
>   light
> Is ever in your smiles.
> To picture out fresh glories, and to cast
> A brighter sunshine o'er our Scottish stage

Epilogue

A loud burst of applause greets the final curtain of *Much Ado About Nothing*. All things considered, this first evening at the Royal Lyceum Theatre has gone extremely well. Few in the audience realise that Ellen Terry is suffering from a cold and even fewer that the wardrobe mistress, after a backstage row, had quit the company at four o'clock that afternoon. Delighted with the performance, the drama critic of *The Scotsman* has already made his notes for tomorrow's edition.

'At times, last night,' he writes of Henry Irving, 'one was tempted to think that Mr Irving's mode of declamation lacked the easy fluency appropriate to Benedick's bantering talk. But, in the main, his rendering left little to be desired; while, alike in dialogue and soliloquy, he so informed his words with racy meaning that any little drawbacks of the kind hinted at were readily forgotten. So it was in regard to action. While it was impossible not to feel that a more graceful style of movement would have better befitted the courtly gallant, yet, so successful was the actor in giving reality to his creation that little attention was left to spare for little oddities of gait or bearing. Whether in speech or in expressive by-play, the veritable Benedick was made to live before us.'

Of Ellen Terry, he is no less fulsome.

'Anything truer in intonation or more gracefully felicitous in gesture and action were hard to conceive; and this phase of her personation may be said to have reached its climax of delicate piquancy in the scene where, having come to call Benedick, she trips off with a coquettish grace well calculated to complete her undreamt-of conquest. Equally exquisite in the expression of womanly tenderness was her rendering of the soliloquy, in which Beatrice resolves that her lover shall not go unrequited; while the colloquy with Benedick where the latter is challenged to avenge the injured Hero, was sustained with a spirit and a picturesque freedom of action that combined with Mr Irving's fine acting to form the crowning triumph of the joint performance.'

The applause intensifies as the curtain rises once more and Henry Irving, leading Ellen Terry by the hand, comes forward to acknowledge the enthusiastic reception the performance has been given. The curtain falls again, then rises to reveal the entire company, plus Mr and Mrs Howard, ranged in a semi-circle on the stage. Led by Miss Kate Sherry and Mr J. Robertson, the National Anthem is sung, followed by much cheering. More cheering follows as Mr Howard leads on the architect, Mr C. J. Phipps, and his assistants — but the greatest cheer of all is heard as Henry Irving steps forward to make the following speech:

> *Irving* Ladies and Gentlemen, — I am sure you believe me when I say to you that I am very glad to be back with you once more. The event of tonight irresistibly reminds me of an event which occurred some twenty-five years ago in Edinburgh, and in which I then took a part. That was the closing night of your old Theatre Royal — a theatre so associated with the traditions of the Scottish stage. Tonight the event is a more cheerful one, and I am sure you will all congratulate my friend Howard on the success of his venture. *(Cheers)* Of course, ladies and gentlemen, we are very much indebted to you for your kind patience tonight. You have exhibited that, especially in the gallery, in a most remarkable manner — *laughter* — knowing, as I am sure you do, the difficulties that we have had to contend with. That accounts for your very kind consideration towards us. You will be sorry to hear that our dilemmas were a little increased at the last moment by the head of one of the departments — and I think it a duty to mention a fact like this — deserting us in our hour of need at four o'clock; therefore we lost a great deal of assistance on that account. With such a delightful theatre as that which Mr Phipps has constructed, with an audience such as an Edinburgh audience is, and with a city such as Edinburgh is to dwell in, I am quite sure

> of the future of those two young managers.
> I rejoice to find that our old friend Robert
> Wyndham's son is one of them — *cheers* —
> I am glad to find that Mr Howard has such
> an earnest fellow-worker and partner. I am
> quite sure that his boat must sail freely both
> with wind and stream.

More cheers and ovations, lasting until past
midnight, whereupon the audience depart. As they
pass through the spacious vestibule, with its mosaic
floor and warm-coloured walls, to the still more
richly decorated foyer, where colossal busts of Mr
Irving and Miss Terry (executed by the artist D. W.
Stevenson) tower above them, and out into the
Edinburgh night, they little realise that, one
hundred years on, the boat is still afloat and sailing
freely.

Index

218